Held Hostage

Courtney,

Thank a lot
for all your
good work

give Freedom

11-11-2022

Arjan Erkel

Held Hostage

"Strength does not come from winning. Your struggles develop your strengths. When you go through hardships and decide not to surrender, that is strength."

-Arnold Schwarzenegger

"It's in the difficult times that we're growing, and you can't just rebuke everything hard. We've got to endure it and fight the good fight of faith and pass the test."

-Joel Osteen

"I will love the light for it shows me the way, yet I will endure the darkness because it shows me the stars."

-Og Mandino

"Victory at all costs, victory in spite of all terror, victory no matter how long and hard the road may be; for without victory, there is no survival."

-Winston Churchill

"You don't know what you're capable of until you have to know what you're capable of."

-David T. Fagan

Praise for Held Hostage

"Arjan's story is the true meaning of a survivor."

-Yurik Mamedov, Paris

"The thoughts, uncertainty, and fear from being kidnapped are as real as if the reader was there."

-Cara, Santa Barbara

"It is a fascinating read of an excruciating story that is presented in a transparent and authentic page-turner."

-Kerry, Florida

"This book is proof of the enduring power of the human spirit."

-Isabel, Arizona

"This book is a great example of hope, faith, and love under extreme circumstances."

-Tyler, Chicago

"No matter what you believe in, this book will have you believing in something bigger than yourself."

-Makenzie, Oregon

Held Hostage

One Man's Story of Trials and Triumph After Being Taken in Dagestan

---

Arjan Erkel

Speaker House Publishing

Special Thanks

The risk associated with writing a word of thanks is that some people might feel neglected. The day after I arrived in the Netherlands, I visited my life coach, Harry Linssen. I asked him, "How can I thank the people who have worked on my release?" Harry answered, "People who have committed themselves to you with unconditional love do not need a thank you."

His words have helped me a lot in most cases. I have never heard family members and real friends ask for an expression of gratitude, but that fact does not mean that I do not want to thank them and have not thanked them. Often, they told me that it was not necessary and that my return was already a gift.

My biggest thanks go to my wife Amina, my parents Dick and Francien, and my brothers, Edger, Diederik, and sister Roos Erkel. They were there for me with loyalty, love, and patience.

I also want to thank Jan Peter Balkenende, Former Prime Minister of the Netherlands, and Ben Bot, former Minister of Foreign Affairs. Without their decisive action, the rebels would not have released me in April 2004. I am grateful for Willem Andreae and Annemarie Ruigrok. They were employees of the Ministry of Foreign Affairs who have worked for my cause.

My respect goes out to Steve and Madina Cornish, Onno Elderenbos, and late Ambassador Tido Hofstee.

I would also like to thank my colleagues from Médecins Sans Frontières, who supported me and wanted the best.

My thanks also go to ice speed skating coach Henk Gemser, who made sure that the KGB veteran's club finally who got me free came into the picture. My thanks also go to the intermediates from that veteran's club. I want to thank the four brave men who risked their lives for me; they were true heroes who put their lives on the line.

It was also a pleasure and honor to read that many politicians, athletes, and actors such as Joe Biden, John McCain, Johan Cruyff, and Angelina Jolie pled for my release.

David Fagan and his team at Speaker House Publishing, I would like to thank them for their input and hard work to finish my book.

Finally, I want to address the many family members, friends, and total strangers in this way. Your e-mails, postcards, and warm words gave me the support I have missed for twenty months. Your attentiveness gave me the energy to feel alive again.

Arjan Erkel

October 2020

Rotterdam

Table of Contents

Chapter 1 Surprise Attack.............................. 1

Chapter 2 No Escape 9

Chapter 3 Blindfold Removed...................... 25

Chapter 4 My Prison Cell.............................. 38

Chapter 5 For Good Behavior...................... 53

Chapter 6 Ramadan 64

Chapter 7 Below Zero 78

Chapter 8 Guard Change 91

Chapter 9 Photoshoot................................. 105

Chapter 10 Counting Down 119

Chapter 11 Letters Home 145

Chapter 12 Just a Few Days........................ 159

Chapter 13 Don't Touch My Gun 170

Chapter 14 The Nobel Rebel 180

Chapter 15 Fear of the Unknown............... 199

Chapter 16 The Television..........................209

Chapter 17 Second Christmas in Captivity. 216

Chapter 18 Questioning My Captors 234

Chapter 19 Hope Brought Life 247

Chapter 20 New News 261

Chapter 21 Man in the Picture 282

Epilogue... 300

x

Freedom is fought against an enemy that never sleeps

Chapter 1

Surprise Attack

Amina said goodbye, and her loving big brown eyes said the rest. I told my girlfriend she would hear from me soon. I turned away and walked through the gate into the dark hours of the evening. I had just said goodbye to her family and her as I had done many times before. Everything seemed as it should be.

Time to wake up the driver Khadji who was sleeping. I got into the white Ford Transit. He rubbed the sleep from his eyes and straightened his seat before starting the engine of the vehicle.

"Did you sleep well?" I asked.

Khadji answered, "No, not really, just listening to some music."

Usually, the driver was also invited to dinner when I visited my girlfriend and her family. This time I asked if he wanted to wait in the car. Not very hospitable, but it was also enjoyable to have no colleagues around me for a while.

We drove from the roadside to the middle of the unpaved street. Another car, without its headlights on, drove onto the sandy path from the roadside. Then the vehicle blinked a few times with the headlight beams. The vehicle stopped across the road and blocked our way. In a flash, three men jumped out of their car and walked towards us. They walked in a V-shape with their arms stretched out and their pistols drawn.

Khadji exclaimed in Russian, "Sto takoye? (What is this now?)" There was no time to answer. I asked myself, why should this happen to me now? I was left to follow my instincts. I exited the vehicle and approached the armed men on autopilot, with no apparent other option. At that moment, it seemed better to me to walk in their direction than to wait until they came to get me out of the car. They came for me and not for the driver. I could be robbed, abducted, or perhaps killed.

Before I realized anything, a fourth assailant hit me from behind with something heavy. I fell on the ground, and the other men started pounding my head with their guns. I curled up in the fetal position, and I used my hands to protect my head. I shouted several times, "I don't speak Russian, I don't understand Russian."

I thought they would beat me to death soon. I kept repeating that I did not speak Russian. Eventually, the answer came, "We don't care." These thugs kept beating on me, and then I saw a baseball bat coming towards me. I had a chance to grab it, and I did. A few extra thumps on my head and right hand made me release the bat. The criminals thought it was enough and dragged me to their car and put me in the back seat between two of them. I was stunned, blood was everywhere on me, and my hand throbbed. I sat there, breathing heavily with a gun to the right side of my head and another gun on the left side of my rib cage.

While I sat there, I heard one of the robbers walking towards my car. I braced myself, wondering if they would shoot Khadji to get rid of any witnesses, but I heard no gunshots. Before they got back in the car, my captors talked with some people.

The kidnappers drove an ordinary car called a Lada. Many Ladas were driving around in Dagestan. We moved backward out of the unpaved alley to the unpaved main street. We were in the suburb of Sputnik in the capital city of Makhachkala. While driving, a scene from Quentin Tarantino's film "Pulp Fiction" ran through my mind. In the movie, John Travolta played casually with his gun. His character accidentally shoots a fellow passenger sitting in the back seat of his car. When the vehicle drives over a speed bump, the gun goes off, and the passenger's brains spread all over the windows and seats. The Russian roads were so bad. I hoped they had seen the scene as well

The first minutes in the car were completely silent. Besides me, the perpetrators seemed to also be in a surreal moment. In the meantime, the blood from my wounds continued to gush down my face. The kidnappers had me bent over with my head between my knees. Breathing heavily, it felt like my heart had reached the end of my arm.

There were four kidnappers, three men around thirty, and one around forty years old. The men in the front seats kept silent. When the gunman on the left calmed down, he searched the pocket of my denim shirt. He found a passport and some business cards. Also, he found five hundred rubles, equal to around twenty US dollars. The thug to my left fished for my keys and a cell phone from my pocket.

My abductors did not find anything else. They allowed me to wear my watch. They asked me, "Where's your gun? Where did you hide your gun?" It was hard for him to imagine that there was no gun. Then the attacker to my left seemed disappointed.

The mugger said to me, "Why do you only have five hundred rubles with you?"

I responded, "Why should I have more with me? You don't need anything else."

He scolded me and said, "What a poor man you are, you can't even go out for dinner." The mugger looked at my passport, read the business cards, and asked me, "Who are those people?" Then he took my old cell phone and found it equally disappointing.

The mugger to my right in the car was a bit friendlier. He pressed a piece of cloth dirty from oil on my head. I thought it was to stop the bleeding and found it surprising that he showed an act of friendliness. Soon he told me it was to protect the car's upholstery.

I recovered from some of the incident's initial shock, but many thoughts still went through my mind. What did all this mean, and how will it end? How will my family, girlfriend, and colleagues react to my abduction? Where are we going?

The mugger to my left asked me aggressively, "Where do you keep your money? How much money is there in the office? What is the monthly revenue? Where are the keys to the office? Are these the keys to the office and the safe?"

For a moment, there was hope. Would this be a robbery? Did they want to drive to the office with me to rob the safe? There was close to $15,000 in cash at the office. I sheepishly told them I did not have an office key. I explained that a coworker lost their access, and management rekeyed the whole place. But the administration had not given me a new key yet. The mood did not get any better in the car. The mugger to the left made it clear that I better not lie or "sell nonsense," as they would say. They made it clear that this would turn out badly for me if I lied.

I got lost in my thoughts again. What do I do? I could not break down. I could not cry, beg, or show any other form of weakness; easier said than done as my mind raced. It was best to speak the truth and lie as little as possible. I knew that the people in Chechnya and Dagestan were tough and liked to act tough. Before we went to the beach, I remember how Amina jokingly suggested how the boys and men behaved on the beach. You would see the boys and men throwing stones as far as possible. Then they wrestled and ran into the Caspian Sea. The boys and men in Dagestan loved to wrestle or engage in other martial arts. They enjoyed sparring with each other. In Russia, the best wrestlers often came from Dagestan.

In my mind, I instinctively came to the next survival strategy. I knew I had to be resilient and have some pride. My abductors would feed on any weakness. But I also had to be realistic about my situation. I had to hope for mercy. I had to ask for mercy. I softly said, "I want to live." Nobody responded to my plea, so I repeated it. "Keep calm," says the mugger on the right. "Nothing will happen to you." I was not sure that I could believe him.

The car traveled quietly further down the dirt road until we turned onto an asphalted road. I tried to keep track of the direction in which we were heading. But I quickly became disoriented and had no idea where we were going.

I came to Dagestan four months ago as Head of Mission for Doctors without Borders Switzerland

(DWB). Several months earlier, I was in Sierra Leone as a project coordinator. My contract was over, and after nine months in West Africa, I wanted something different. I chose to work in Dagestan out of love for the people and to build my career.

Dagestan, a sub-republic of the Russian Federation in the North Caucasus, is located next to Chechnya. A civil war had existed for years between the Chechnya Islam fighters and Russia. Russia did not allow an independent Chechnya. Doctors without Borders received Chechen refugees fleeing the civil war.

I used to work in the former Soviet Union, and I liked it. I learned to speak Russian, and I always enjoyed my years in Tajikistan and Uzbekistan. I had dealt with refugee issues before, and maybe I would like it here as much as in Central Asia.

Another reason I chose Dagestan as a duty assignment was Amina, my fiancée. Her family is originally from Dagestan, and they just moved back. This position would be good for the relationship, and it would push me forward in my career.

The Head of Mission duties included oversight of the:

- Safety Department
- Human Resources Department
- Finance Department
- Logistics Department
- Local Relations Department

Dagestan had a varied population. In total, there were more than 30 different ethnic groups, each with their distinct language. All the ethnic groups spoke Russian. DWB's personnel policy attempted to take demographics into account. DWB's personnel reflected the demographics of the population.

In Dagestan, the programs consisted of two mobile medical teams. We provided for unregistered refugees unable to rely on government health care. We installed sanitary facilities and supplied the refugees with some building material. Clothing and a bridge class for the children made the program complete.

While working in Chechnya, you ran the risk of abduction by Muslim rebel fighters. I had been to Chechnya about five times, and each time it was a tense situation. We had to wait until the Russian army cleared the main road. The rebels often laid land mines down at night. I remembered how we were once unexpectedly stopped and ordered to get out of our vehicle. The heavily armed Russian soldiers searched the car and us.

Security was not the only problem in Chechnya. The threat of abduction was also a possibility in Dagestan. Organized crime and political tensions in Dagestan had risen sharply in recent years. Someone could quickly end up in the wrong place at the wrong time. All the warnings were there. Now it had become a painful reality. The hurt was real, and it was just beginning.

Chapter 2

No Escape

After a one-hour drive, my hope for a robbery disappeared for good. The car turned off the main road and drove into the hills. Not too far from the country road, the kidnappers told me to get out of the car and start walking into the mountains. The first thing that struck me was that it was quite cold. The kidnappers recommended that I did not even think about escaping. They did not wear masks, but they reminded me that it was better if I did not see their faces. Walking up the steep hill was quite tricky. I was wearing shoes with slippery leather soles. We walked for about ten minutes before arriving at a place where we stayed the first night. It was a place covered with tall grass and shrubs on the slope of one of the hills. Two of the four abductors stayed with me; the other two disappeared.

The kidnappers interrogated me and warned me, "If you lie, we will shoot you." They sounded serious.

They asked, "Why did you pretend you did not speak Russian when we picked you up?"

That was already the first lie, but I could correct it.   I did not want to die because of miscommunication.

They continued, "Who were you visiting?"

Furthermore, they wanted to know why I came to Dagestan.   What DWB wanted in return for their help.   They did not understand the concept of humanitarian aid.   They could not believe Doctors Without Borders did not want anything in return. They wanted to know, "How can you leave the driver outside when you ate with the family?   Not very hospitable, a Dagestani would never do such a thing!"

They asked, "Why did you try to flee?"   They told me they had to beat me up, and it was my fault that I covered the back seat of the car with my blood.

I asked about my driver.   They shared with me that he was savagely beaten but left alive.   This fact gave me great relief!

I suppressed my curiosity and gaze while talking to my kidnappers.   Acting uninterested was incredibly difficult when the conversation stopped for a moment.

In my wildest dreams, I never thought about my kidnapping and what the experience would entail.   I made all my colleagues read and sign the security regulations, and now I was going through them in my mind.

Some of the regulations stated:

- Do not give the kidnappers a reason to use force against you.
- Avoid eye contact.
- Do not talk about politics and religion.
- In case of liberation by force, make sure you lay down on the floor with your head covered with your hands.
- Do not panic!

My abductors knew that they had me under their control, and I felt confident that I must not resist. It was better to wait and see how the situation developed. I saw a clear sky and many shooting stars. I made a "wish on a star" about staying alive. Over time they tied my feet with one of their straps. Then they threatened to shoot me through my knees if I tried to escape. Just to be sure, they added, "We have seen enough death and destruction, so shooting you does nothing to us." I answered, "I will not try to escape." The relatively pleasant kidnapper removed the dirty rag from my swollen hand. My injured head throbbed with the rhythm of my heart. Adrenaline killed the pain. He also looked at my wounds on my head and promised to buy medicines and pain killers the next day. He improvised a pillow from leaves and advised me to sleep.

I did not panic, but a sort of resignation came over me. Let me behave calmly and just wait and see what happens. The kidnapping seemed professional. Why don't those guys drive me directly to a house?

What am I doing here in the hills? Are they going to bury me here? They would have shot me long ago, right? The behavior of the abductors reassured me to a certain extent. They needed me alive.

I did not get much sleep. I felt cold, uncomfortable, and too tense. The first mental inconveniences of the abduction played out. I needed to pee, but with two armed men nearby, this was exceedingly difficult. First, they thought that I was trying to seize this moment to escape, and second, I had shy bladder syndrome, a social disorder. At night I wondered several times why I was not at home lying in my bed as planned. My boss in Geneva, my team, and I, all were so wrong in our judgments.

One week ago, on August 6, our Khasavyurt office received a call from our contact person at the FSB (Federalnaya Sluzhba Bezopasnosti). The FSB is a successor agency of the Soviet-era KGB and is the internal security service in Russia. The contact person said there was a significant risk of abduction for foreign aid workers. DWB was the only foreign aid organization in Dagestan. It seemed evident to me that it was a threat. I took the warning seriously and called the team back from Khasavyurt. I decided that only Hakan, Mauricio, and I would stay behind in Makhachkala. We evacuated the other foreign staff members.

The Lieutenant Colonel of police advised me to stay indoors in the evening and not walk on the street alone. Also, he offered me armed guards. I explained to him that armed guards did not fit within the DWB policy. He suggested a civilian officer. I also rejected that. I did agree with his offer for extra surveillance around the office and the houses.

The day after, FSB welcomed us. They recommended armed surveillance. Again, I explained that humanitarian help and armed, uniformed oversight were not consistent.

Mauricio and I drove to Khasavyurt on Friday. We hoped to speak to the mayor and head of the province. The mayor made time and noticed something that made me think.

"If the warning comes from the FSB, it could be a provocation."

I tried to reach the agent that informed us about the possible danger. We even went to his office, but he refused to see us.

Experienced colleagues and local staff also did not know what to do with the warning. DWB had often received notices without anything happening.

Earlier in the day, Mauricio and I met the political head of the Khasavyurt province. He told us crime had returned to the region. In the afternoon, Mauricio and I had lunch with the hospital director in the Chechen city of Gudermes. This man was one of the most critical contacts from Chechnya for the team. He also did not see any reason for alarm.

Late afternoon we drove back to Makhachkala. After the busy and charged day, I did not feel like cooking or eating out with the team members. I preferred a quiet evening with Amina's family. The family gathering went well.

Instead of lying in bed, I sat in the hills, not too far from the city, waiting anxiously. At first light, we climbed another foothill. We stopped at a better shelter. No one talked. The weather was nice and clear. In the south, I saw an asphalt road with some traffic. Sometimes I heard the droning sound of an airplane engine in the distance. If a helicopter flew nearby, I had to hide in the bushes. I hoped the authorities started a search

I did not understand what we were doing there. Was it a kidnapping or not? Maybe it was a final warning. Perhaps they wanted to make it clear to me that it was best to leave Dagestan. In my mind's eye, I saw Amina's eyes saying goodbye. I hoped to be left alone with one kidnapper to increase the odds of overpowering him. It had been quiet for a while. I looked back and saw the legs of the second man lying in the sun to my disappointment.

"Look in front of you," he recommended. "If you are hungry, I have some cookies."

With his gun pointed at me, I grabbed the roll of cookies without looking at him. I had to go to the toilet, but I was embarrassed to ask. Eventually, I could not stop it anymore. I took my first humiliating walk into the bushes. The guy stood behind me while I sat with my trousers down around my ankles. To make it worse, I heard him loading his gun.

One gangster returned late in the afternoon with grilled chicken in aluminum foil. Also, he brought a package with him.

He said to me, "Here you have some chicken."

I told him, "Thanks."

"At least you remain a gentleman," he said with irony in his voice.

At nightfall, we walked up the hill. They unpacked the package, and it was a tent.

He said, "You go and lie in the tent. You must be cold."

It did indeed cool down quickly, and the tent provided warmth and privacy. My abductors gave me painkillers, some anti-infection powder, a bandage, and even returned my passport.

The kidnappers said that they had been following me for a month before they struck. They came after me because they figured I was the boss. They wanted an enormous ransom.

The kidnappers continued to interrogate me like they did the first night. They asked me, "Is the Netherlands a rich country?" "How much money does DWB have?" "What does your father do for a living?" "Is your father rich? "Does he have a house that he can sell?" They tried to figure out how much I was worth.

They asked, "What's the name of the man from DWB who got abducted last year?" I answered his name was Kenny Gluck. He got abducted in 2001 for twenty-six days. My kidnappers heard that a fifteen million ransom was paid. I told him that he was released without paying. They did not believe me. "No one is leaving without a ransom being paid."

I asked my captors, "How much are you going to ask for me?" They wanted to ransom me for twelve million. When I told them that it was way too much, they asked me what I thought was the right amount. I was perplexed. What to say to them? Too low might be dangerous. I told them one million. First, they disagreed. But a little later, they said that, although they preferred five million, one million was also a nice sum.

The interrogation continued, "Are you a spy? How come you did not have a weapon in your pocket? Did you leave the weapon in the car?"

The kidnappers set aside the thought that I did not have a weapon. They wanted to know what the Dutch secret service was looking for in Dagestan. They believed that someone from the West had ulterior motives. I understood their line of thinking. People in the former Soviet often suspected DWB of espionage. This idea stemmed from older people and people working for security services. They thought all foreigners were spies, especially journalists and social workers. Who else works in such dangerous places?

Although I continued to deny the allegations, I could not change the kidnapper's minds. Finally, I said, "Then prove that I am a spy." I tried to reverse the situation.

They continued the interrogation for a while longer. "Have you not noticed that we have followed you? Who were the others in the van? Who were those young ladies? What did you want in the town hall?" They thought it was strange that, as an experienced spy, I did not notice them shadowing me almost all day.

The questioning continued, "Did you not see the other cars surveilling you? Were you asleep or something? Don't you ever look in your rear or side mirror? We followed you, and guys in two other Lada's followed you. They were watching when we kidnapped you, and they congratulated us. We were just too fast for them." I asked in surprise, "Is that so?"

They answered with, "Be glad we abducted you and not them. Those were evil criminals, and you would have a much harder time."

I wondered where the two abductors would sleep. When night fell, they also entered the tent. They told me, "Turn around and don't look at us."

The three of us slept in the small double tent. I slept peacefully enough.

The long wait started the next day. I was in the tent, and the men were outside. They played with their weapons. They took out the bullets, cleaned the guns, and performed a check with the gun empty. It was intimidating.

The kidnappers spoke a language unknown to me—the many throaty sounds made while speaking did not sound like Chechen. Occasionally they involved me in their conversations. I am lucky to speak Russian; otherwise, I would have nothing to do at all.

The interrogation continued yet another day. They asked, "What kind of gun do you normally have with you? What was the best hand weapon among you? How much does a gun cost you?" They tried again with all their questions. I told them the prices of guns I had read in our newspapers in Rotterdam.

Their other favorite subjects were sports, cars, and yes, women. Whether I had ever done a Dagestani woman? How often could I do it in one night? What kind of car did I have, and what was my favorite car?

Their ideal was, of course, the Mercedes-600. The Mercedes-600 was a real status symbol in Dagestan. At that time, I had bought an old Volvo for 400 dollars because I lived abroad. I gave it to my friend Olaf when I left for Russia. They saw this as if I were trying to lower my ransom again.

They said that they had been walking around for years with the idea of abducting a foreigner. "We had the right help, everything was well organized, and we could proceed with our kidnapping. We just care about the money!" After a moment of silence, he continued, "We had already devised a plan to take you out of the house."

I parried, "As if I would just open the door for you?"

He responded, "We had already thought of that. We wanted to have a beautiful woman ring the bell, and you would have opened the door. She could have possibly overpowered you with a sleeping aid and let us in."

During the moments left alone, I thought of the misery that my parents and my colleagues now had to endure. How would my mother receive the news? My grandmother had her first heart attack around sixty-three. If only my mother did not get a heart attack when she heard the news. Or even my father, although he was physically stronger. My sister had imagined a much different 25th birthday. I remembered a beautiful ceramic plate that I had made for her in Uzbekistan. The news about my kidnapping was not much like a present.

During the conversations, I needed all my concentration not to say the wrong things. When we were silent, I felt physical problems. My hand hurt. I could not stretch my middle finger anymore. The blood in my hair felt dirty, and the crusts on my wounds felt dirty and unpleasant.

There was nothing to eat or drink. The romance of camping without facilities had evaporated. It remained humiliating to squat with an armed kidnapper standing a few meters behind me. The absence of water did not make things better.

Despite the misery, I was happy that I had been kidnapped and not a colleague. Like an army leader from earlier times, the boss should take the lead, even in times of adversity. If these thugs had abducted someone else, it would have been a more significant defeat. I had talked to colleagues and Amina about the chance of being abducted. We assumed that there was more risk in Khasavyurt than in Makhachkala. Khasavyurt was on the border with Chechnya.

They brought me grilled chicken with bread, fresh cucumber, and a bit of water in the evening. In the city, street vendors sold grilled chicken. I did not know the location of our campsite, but the town was not far away!

My guards alternated during the day. The two abductors from the back seat alternated with the two from the front seat. They brought me food. Besides Dagestan pancakes filled with cheese or meat, they gave me yogurt.

They told me, "If you can look in front of you and behave, you can sit outside. It will be too warm in the tent." I agreed to behave. I sat in front of the tent while they were one and a half meters from me. I looked straight ahead and saw an occasional car down in the valley. Also, an occasional helicopter or plane flew over. We were not far from the airport! After dark, I saw some lights from a city in the distance. I heard a sound that resembled a ship's horn. One of the kidnappers told me, "That is Izberbazj south of Kaspiysk."

He said, "Do you know Thomas?"

I responded, "Yes, I know several."

One Thomas flew from Geneva to Moscow and was even planning to come to Dagestan. The operational director and general director were both named Thomas. The news gave me hope. Maybe the negotiations about my ransom had started. They also told me that Khadji, my driver, was detained for three days as a suspect but was now free again.

On Friday, I heard them praying for the first time. So, their devoutness as Muslims came into question. We had more water on Friday. They shared a sample bottle of shampoo with me. I finally washed the blood out of my hair. Water was now available for washing after using the bush as a toilet. The atmosphere was less tense. They did not stand behind me anymore.

During dinner, they asked my opinion on the food. The kidnappers wanted to know if I liked it. I told them that the chicken tasted quite delicious, but I had not yet eaten the 20-dollar meal. They appreciated the joke and said that it costs much more than that altogether.

I asked, "How long will we stay here?" They shared with me, "We are arranging a different place, but it needs more preparation."

There was still not much water—my blood-stained shirt stank of sweat. For the umpteenth time, I thought it would be nice to take a shower or swim in the sea.

On Sunday evening, the gangsters announced that they would probably hand me over to a new gang the next day. They informed me, "Then you get your room in an apartment." That sounded at least normal. Maybe I could have a private toilet and who knows, perhaps a TV!

Monday afternoon, the news came that the exchange would happen. I asked, "How does the exchange work?" They told me someone would drive me blindfolded to the apartment.

I traded my white T-shirt for a black T-shirt from the oldest abductor. When we exchanged shirts, he indicated that the shirt stinks. Not so strange after a week without soap and water.

Then the kidnapper who was the friendliest blindfolded me with two rolls of bandage. He said,

"Don't worry too much. People from DWB have already flown in to meet you. We made contact already. If all goes well, you will be home again in two months." This news sounded like music to my ears! An average abduction in the North Caucasus took six to seven months; then, two months were not so bad.

While one of the gangsters held me around my waist with my belt, we walked down the slope. Because of my leather shoes, I could not walk fast enough for them.

I felt nervous. What kind of new gang will it be? Will something happen on the way? How do we get past all the block posts in the city? What if a shooting occurs at one of the police posts?

Down the hill, a car waited for us. I could not see the kind of car. But I thought it was a Lada. The new man wanted my passport, so I gave it to him. We drove quite fast on asphalted roads. After about ten minutes, my neighbor slid the passport under my right thigh. Occasionally we left the main road and went on country roads. It seemed to me our erratic route allowed us to bypass the block posts. I tried to orient myself. In the car, everyone stayed dead silent with tension.

I wondered if this would be my last ride?!!

The car stopped after more than an hour of fast driving. I felt like we were standing in front of an old four-story apartment building on the edge of a not too big city. Of course, this feeling was my imagination. I wondered if a psychologist could explain my mind and my emotions. The place in my mind might even match with where I should be according to my orientation. In the meantime, two kidnappers I knew came to sit next to me. A new man sat in the passenger seat. It still seemed like I was not wearing a blindfold and saw him as a man with dark wild hair. With increased tension, we drove away again. The car stopped after about ten minutes. The man with the crazy bunch of hair exited the vehicle and returned after a minute of stress. He ordered me to be quiet!

It seemed to me that a guard guided him through a block post and that we headed for the next one. He shouted in a hoarse bass voice, "Lie down at the bottom, lie down at the bottom!" I laid down with my stomach on the floor behind the front seats. I could not stretch out my legs with some of my weight distributed on my face. I felt a barrel of a revolver on my head. Still blindfolded, "wild hair" beat me as he turned around. He hit me more out of nervousness than sadism. All the others were calm. The neighbor on the left removed my shoes and placed them next to me. We drove on a rough road for about ten minutes. I believed we passed the tunnel on the way to the south of Dagestan. I had only been on that road once, but I thought we were there.

Chapter 3
Blindfold Removed

It was dark when we arrived at the location where the kidnappers transferred me to the new group. One of the kidnappers taunted, "Have fun in your apartment." I squeezed out of the car while someone led me by my hand. He introduced himself, but I was so tense that I did not remember his name. I asked him to bring my shoes from the car. He told me to sit down, and I looked at the ground and put my hand on my forehead. A ritual I had learned the first week of captivity. I sat there for about five minutes without being addressed. Strangely enough, I felt uninhibited because I surrendered control, or did a life and death situation activate self-preservation? I did not have another choice.

A man came up to me and asked in a friendly way, "Why do not you dare to look at us? Do you sometimes suffer from the light? Have you been blindfolded all week?"

I carefully looked up and saw two stocky men and a taller man. All had balaclavas on their faces and wore camouflage uniforms. I saw strings of hand grenades around their waists. Did I end up in the hands of the Russian army? But then I noticed that the men did not wear badges. Anyone can buy Russian uniforms at the market and shops. Some Russian soldiers sell their weapons and uniforms to the rebels.

The man introduced himself again as General. He said he was the leader of a group of Chechen fighters. He wanted to have my passport.

It was hard to believe we were in Chechnya. In my opinion, we had not driven that far. There was also a curfew in Chechnya, and I did not think it was possible to go on the main roads at night. General left me for a moment. I was alone with the two stocky men. Although they wore masks, I saw their inquisitive and curious looks in their eyes. They reminded me of ostriches that also turn their heads and necks.

I heard a river and saw a gravel pit somewhere high up in the mountains, and I did not see any apartment buildings. I saw the lights of a village behind me in the valley. Perhaps there were flats in the town. General came back with another man in a camouflage uniform and asked, "Are you healthy? Can you walk?".

From the river, we ascended into the mountains. We walked up along narrow paths and deep canyons. We followed small animal tracks, and now and then, we had to climb over rocks. My leather soles were slippery. I felt afraid that I might fall. My captors did not want to lose 5 million dollars. They looked after me.

After a couple of hours, we stopped our hike. I did not see anything that looked like an apartment. I needed privacy and comfort. The General pointed to a hole in the ground and said, "This is the toilet."

I was confused. Then the ground started to move, and a hidden door opened. Another fighter gestured me to enter the place. Under the soil, they had dug out a hiding place. I had to take my shoes off. I walked bent over for a couple of yards until I entered an underground room with a kitchen, sink, and a stove. Pots, pans, and food laid on the shelves.

The five men were silent, and they looked me over curiously. I felt calm and curious about what was coming next. General orders, "Take a shower. You smell bad!" I retreated with a candle to a small bathroom with a French toilet. There were a stool and a bucket of warm water with shampoo, soap, and a sponge. I should not make a mess in their little bathroom. With the door closed, it was the first moment of privacy. Even though it was not an apartment, it felt like luxury. I had not been able to brush my teeth because there was no toothbrush for me. I was afraid to ask for a toothbrush. Maybe they would beat me up, causing me to lose my teeth, so I don't have to brush them anymore. If I did not ask, my teeth would rot.

Me: "General, do you have some toothpaste for me?"

General: "Which brand do you want?"

Me: "I use Aquafresh at home."

General: "Aquafresh? I never heard of that but will try to buy it for you."

When clean, they gave me used underpants, an army T-shirt, and a new green Adidas tracksuit. It was already midnight, and I had to go straight to my place to sleep. I slept in the room with the rebels against the wall, furthest away from the door. Three fighters laid their sleeping bags parallel to mine, and one rebel slept at our feet.

It was a room of four by four meters (13 feet by 13 feet). The fighters covered the walls, floor, and ceiling of their underground hideout with plywood. They put carpet on the floor, and the room was approximately twenty centimeters (8 inches) lower than the corridor. Their shelter had an open doorway with the atmosphere of an army barracks. There were weapons, army backpacks, and camouflage clothing hanging on hooks. Also, they had some shelves with books and videos. In the corner, there was a television with a video player. Strangely there was no electricity. The light came from a candle near the door. Next to the candle was a rebel, probably the night guard. We crawled into our sleeping bags, and the revolutionaries did not take their balaclavas off. I fell asleep right away.

Early in the morning, they woke me up. Someone shouted, "Otvernish!" I did not know what it meant. "Otvernish !!!" I had to turn my face to the wall. The men stood behind me and shuffled back and forth. As I looked at the wall, I heard the men moving, their clothes rustling. They shouted unintelligible cries, and they breathed heavily. I felt like a lamb going to the slaughter! Were they going to slit my throat? Must I flee? I felt all my power slip away. Would this be the end of me? As it turned out, it was just their morning prayer. I had the misfortune of being between them and Mecca. They put my face against the wall because they wanted to pray without masks.

"Stand up!" One of the rebels ordered me to follow him to the kitchen. He gave me a plate with salad and bread and handed me a cup of tea. In the big room, I was not allowed to look at their weapons. In the kitchen, I could not look at the cooking knives.

The kitchen was about two by three meters (6.5 feet by 10 feet). Black and white linoleum covered the floor. There was also a home-made low table and some short stools without backs. The man was a stocky 5 feet 5 inches, and his mask irritated him, and he scratched his face. His appearance intimidated me, and he tried to start a conversation. He asked, "Are your parents still alive? Do you have brothers and sisters?" He did not respond when I asked him questions. Maybe I should just be quiet.

He had an old gun in his holster. Suddenly he pointed his gun at my face and pulled the trigger. I heard a dry click. He said, "Just kidding."

General blindfolded me and put handcuffs on me. He brought me outside, where we sat down in the shade of a tree. He quietly explained to me again that I was in the hands of a group of Chechen rebels. This hideout offered temporary refuge for insurgents who wanted to recover from fighting. He told me he had nothing to do with my kidnapping. He heard about it on the radio before being asked to guard me. He said, "The house is not yet ready to receive you, but we will prepare a room for you as soon as possible." His words were quite convincing.

The men were not only rebels but also Muslims. General did not want to attach a fundamentalist or Wahabi label to it. But he explained that they strictly follow the Quran and sunnah of Prophet Muhammad. He told me, "The Quran was the word of God revealed to Muhammad. God bestowed His soul and peace upon Muhammad by the Archangel Gabriel. Muhammad recorded the revelations. The sunnah is precepts taught by Muhammad. We also take the way Muhammad lived his life as an example." He explained, "As an austere Muslim, he had no problem with abductions. The Prophet took civilians hostage when he wanted to conquer Mecca. We do not direct your abduction against you personally, nor Doctors without Borders. We just want to earn money in this way to buy weapons to fight the Russians." According to General Russia:

- Invaded without provocation.
- Violated the sovereignty of Chechnya.
- Tried to force their infidel culture upon the people in Chechnya.

He had studied the Quran and reference works on the life of Muhammad. He had not found how to deal with hostages. But he found in his religious studies how to deal with prisoners. General learned, "He must treat prisoners well if they behaved well."

General laid out these rules, "You will get to eat whatever we eat. If you are hungry, just to tell us you will get more. There is plenty of water and tea to drink. Unfortunately, not unlimited water to wash. You can wash and brush your teeth twice a day and shower once a week. I already told my men they should treat you normally."

I listened quietly. The General did not seem unfriendly. If his men treated me according to his rules, I would manage the coming two months. General told me, "If you obey us, we will treat you well. If you try to flee, we will kill you without any hesitation. Are you someone like Schwarzenegger? I do not think so. In the real world, one bullet is enough for experienced fighters like us."

'I have discussed it with a friend, and he told me that it sometimes might take longer than a year. I hope it doesn't take so long." General answered my question about how long he thinks it will last. He also estimated my worth in ransom at five million dollars. I had little doubt about DWB and how they would deal with my case. They had experience with other abductions in the region. They had been working in the Caucasus for years. They knew the culture and understood how to deal with kidnapping. I hoped they would support my parents. I also hoped that the media would cover my case. I did not want to be left alone or forgotten.

Just like the kidnappers, General wanted to know how rich DWB was. He wanted to know how much money my parents had. He wished to know if the Netherlands was a rich country. Was it true that I was Jewish and a spy and a "master of sport in boxing?" I had told the kidnappers that I boxed from the age of sixteen to twenty-two. I denied all the assertions, but General did not believe my denial. I just left it that way. Maybe they would respect me. I was also almost twenty centimeters (8 inches) taller than most of them.

They did not believe that I was not a Jew and a spy. They were satisfied that I was not an American. My captors told me, "We hate Americans. If you were American, we would make it difficult for you."

We somehow started to talk about the exchange and about the man who beat me. I told General of the cowardly act by the Chechen that beat me while defenseless. General found the beating cowardly too. He told me the kidnappers had nothing to do with his group. He said his people did not behave like that.

The next morning the same guy as yesterday prepared me breakfast. In my mind, I called him Povar, which means "cook" in Russian. He was still not hospitable and pointed his gun at me a few more times. Maybe I should just call him John Wayne.

After breakfast, I asked General if he wanted to shave my head. Due to the lack of washing opportunities, it seemed more hygienic if I was completely bald. General shaved me carefully. After shaving my head, he even spread zeljonka, Russian green iodine, on my wounds. It was a moment of intimacy, and I felt protection in his behavior.

In the night, a new guard showed up. He was a big, cheerful guy with a big belly and whistled when he saw my swollen hand. He applied a bandage around my hand and put a splint on my finger.

"Call me Kavkazki Krest," he said. Caucasian Cross instead of the Red Cross.

I said, "Then call me, Baltimor." Kavkazki Krest looked at me in surprise. I referred to a famous Russian advertisement from ketchup manufacturer Baltimor. The father at the dinner table gives the tag line, "Tell him (Baltimor) he is always the most welcome guest at the table."

I said, "From now on, I am your most welcome guest. You have to take good care of me because I will bring you a lot of money."

That afternoon it started to rain, and they brought me inside. In the kitchen, the grumpy man became a little less cranky when Kavkazki Krest joined him. I told the cook that we had nicknames for each other and that I also have one for him, Povar. He was not enthusiastic.

Because of the rain, I spent the whole day in the big room with one or two guards looking after me. The others were still building my room. They gave me a book: *The Divine Miracles, Testimonials of the Existence of Allah.* Maybe they wanted to increase my knowledge about Islam so that I would convert. I left the book, untouched.

I got to know my guards little by little. It helped that we were together in one room. I once read that it was best to build a relationship to become more challenging for them to kill you. I studied them and hoped they would talk to me.

The guards did not have much compassion. They said indifferently, "Everyone faced difficulties these days. Lots of people got kidnapped."

In the beginning, I thought their words did not make sense because if they were in my position, they would feel different. After some rethinking, I came to a different conclusion. I did not know them and did not know what they had experienced. They thought I had it easy. I told myself that my situation was not so bad. I knew examples where the hostage's fingers and ears were cut off, where they were raped, and barely given anything to eat. I was thinking of my family at home. What kind of images did they see in their imagination?

Although they did not abuse or terrorize me, they were still enormously suspicious. I wondered why did my captors think of me as a spy and Jewish. Maybe someone fed them fake information.

I had the most significant difficulty with the outdoor latrine. It was the hole in the ground that General pointed out to me when we arrived.

The problem was that I had to do number two with two guards standing right behind me. The guards call the toileting "Visiting Putin." The Russian President promised in 1999 that he would "kill all Chechen rebels! Even if they had to pursue them into the restrooms." Putin had to wait four days for me to come to see him. At the toilet, the guard removed the handcuffs and blindfold. But in the meantime, the urge disappeared. I had to get used to it. In two months, I only had to endure this humiliation fifteen times.

With masks and their army outfits, the guards looked the same. I started to recognize subtle differences. Tank was my name for a small, very stocky man who paced back and forth all the time. He gave the impression that it was impossible to stop him if he went mad. Tank told me that all his family died during the first war in Chechnya. He saw no reason to continue living. Tank studied law, but due to the war, he was unable to finish.

Tank: "How old do you think I am?"

I had some difficulty answering. Should I just say something, or should I try to guess it? Knowing too much was not good but turning around the obvious was probably not good either. It would not help my credibility, and that was what I was building up just now. I estimated him at twenty-eight.

Tank: "You are not stupid. How did you deduce that?"

Of course, I did not know if I was right. But I told Tank that I reckoned from his student days during the first war in 1994 until now. And that his way of talking and asking also told me something about his age. His wish was to perish as quickly as possible in the war. He wanted to go to heaven as a martyr. He was not an unfriendly person.

Professor was the tallest of all the men. I saw him reading a lot, and he had a somewhat broader general knowledge and interest than the others. I saw his dark beard occasionally under his mask. He sang the Azan, the call to Muslim prayer, and read from the Quran.

The first Saturday, General, Tank, and I were sitting in the room. General was cleaning his gun.

Me: "Who is going to kill me?"

General shot a hole in the wall just above Tank's head with a massive flash of light and a big bang.

36

General: "Me."

Tank and I reacted impassively. I expected Tank to say something about it. General was disappointed that he did not scare me.

General: "How come you stayed so calm? At least I expected you to do it in your pants."

Me: "I had experienced a few things in Tajikistan and Sierra Leone and was not so easily impressed anymore."

After a week, my cell was ready. The rebel fighters dug my prison cell between the kitchen and the big room. General gathered everyone to dedicate the space. For the occasion, he gave me a military hat that Fidel Castro often wore. He explained the house rules one more time. As good Muslims, they must treat their prisoner well. No beating or calling names. I was fed twice a day and could always ask for more if I was still hungry. After I ate, I could wash and brush my teeth. If I had to go to the toilet, the guards must take me outside. They also had to clean the floor in my room. House rule number one was "no escaping, or they would shoot me dead."

Me: "Beautiful loft, well done. Who is the architect?"

General: "I am; who else."

I was relieved that I had a room for myself. But of course, I was far from happy.

Chapter 4
My Prison Cell

The "initiation" of my room soon came to an end. The guards walked out of the room, and the door closed. After two weeks, I finally had some privacy. The fear of misconduct by the guards had diminished. But I wondered if having a room was an improvement.

For the first time during my abduction, I had a lock on my door. With my cap on, I stood still before the step to the door. I looked at the ceiling with my teeth and lips pressed tightly together. I felt small, exceedingly small. I looked at the ceiling beams and the walls, large, thick beams, and short, thin posts. They faded together after a few moments, and I took my first step.

The room was small, only 5 feet by 6.5 feet. There was a small extension where the door could open inside. The door was about 5 feet high. They had lowered the ceiling and the floor in front of the door, so I could not run into the door and force it open.

If I stood up straight, my head touched the ceiling. They nailed my bed to the wall at 3 feet high on a wooden board. It covered up about 6.5 feet by 3 feet of space. That left me less than 22 square feet to maneuver. There were two shelves on the wall where I could put the two candles they gave me. I had a wooden floor. Plywood covered the first 3 feet of the walls.

Beams of gray light trickled under the door and through an air duct. From now on, I lived in permanent twilight. It smelled nice, like a pine forest. I searched for a weakness somewhere in the wall or the ceiling so that I could try to escape one day. The upright trunks were clamped around the ceiling by a rectangle of thicker boxes. That made an angle of ninety degrees with the other boxes. It was impossible to move them.

I walked around a bit, although walking around was an exaggeration, two long steps, and that was all. To make my room seem larger, I decided to take four small steps. If I turned too fast, the motion made me nauseous. So, I decided to walk the figure eight.

They gave me a small stool too large for my large frame from the kitchen. It was not comfortable. I decided to lie down on the bed on top of my sleeping bag. There was no mattress. Would lying in bed be my future pastime?

During my extensive studies and in my free time, I gained a good foundation in Islam. Even with nothing to do at all, I still did not want to read "Divine Miracles." My captor's religion allowed kidnappings in the name of God. How could they think I was interested to learn more about their faith at this moment?

I started to count the days since my abduction. Fourteen days had passed. I figured my release would happen on the 15th of October, two months and a few days from my kidnapping. By my calculation, I only had 50 days left.

I woke up the first night by an attack of claustrophobia. I tried to breathe calmly, but it did not work very well. It was very dark in my room. I had no matches, and I could not open the door myself. I could not relax, but I did not dare disturb the guards. It was better not to "wake sleeping dogs." After much consideration, I knocked on the door to ask for matches.

It appeared to be no problem for me to have some matches. They said, "One of us is always awake at night to watch everything. Please do not burn the house."

In the morning, I laid on my bed, thinking, and sat on my stool a bit. In short, there was enough time to think about anything and everything. I did push-ups and a lot of ab exercises. Amina could be proud of me later. I survived a kidnapping, and I would look like an Adonis. It was a good time to lose some weight.

I had to pee. I knocked on the door to see how fast the guard would react. A guard came immediately, and he led me outdoors to the privy.

I did not eat with the security guard in the kitchen anymore. They passed me my food by way of a hatch in the door. I got a spoon, plastic glass, and stainless-steel soup plate.

General: "We do not want you to infect us with some contagious disease. We have scoured the sharp side of the spoon so that you cannot use it as a stabbing weapon."

After the hot food, a guard knocked on my door and asked, "Umivatcha khochesh," or "Do you want to wash?" I could brush my teeth and got a red plastic jug with one and a half liters of water.

They purchased "Aquafresh" and a genuine Oral-B-Plus toothbrush for me, and I could tell that Povar was even a little jealous. He showed me his toothbrush and toothpaste.

Povar: "What about this brand? Is this real or stampovka?"

You could buy counterfeit products in Russia. The markets in Russia sold counterfeit clothing, videos, and CDs. Counterfeit goods were called "stampovka."

His toothpaste was apparently of lesser quality.

Me: "You can try my toothpaste."

He was surprised at the difference.

Povar: "Now, I understand why you have white teeth."

After brushing my teeth and washing, I had to go back to my room. I took my toothpaste to my room. Otherwise, the guards would use it up.

In the afternoon, I had time to think and work on my physique. I knocked on the door again to see how quickly the guard would respond. They whisked me off to the toilet with no problem. In the evening, they brought soup with bread. After dinner, I washed and brushed my teeth again.

The first day in my room was over. The boredom and monotony frightened me more than injury or loneliness. Boredom and monotony were my greatest enemies.

I also had to be careful that I did not neglect myself. I had read that hostages who got stuck for a long time skip their hygiene and eat less. I had to prevent becoming one of them. I had to control my aggression and be careful not to provoke anything. It would only work against me if I lost my temper.

My imprisonment had lasted for a few days now, and a certain regularity was starting to emerge. The guards centered their daily life around a prayer schedule. As good Muslims, they prayed at least five times a day at the prescribed times. I had learned that in the beginning, Allah wanted the Prophet Muhammad to pray to Him many more times. But

Muhammad asked Allah to reduce the number of prayers to work and take care of his family.

The first time to pray was supposed to be just before sunrise. Before praying, I heard a lot of walking back and forth to the little bathroom at the end of the kitchen. The guards ritually cleaned themselves before they participated in the prayer. One of the guards, usually Professor, sang the azan and called on everyone to follow him in prayer. My room was next to the guard's room, and I did not have soundproofed walls. To me, the azan sounded like my alarm clock, my good friend Olaf gave me.

After praying, it was time for breakfast. I preferred to skip breakfast and sleep as long and as much as possible so that the days would go by faster. I only ate yogurt in the morning anyway.

General urged me to eat breakfast because it was healthy. He bought me fruit yogurt. I took the yogurt to my room every evening after washing to enjoy it the next morning. At least the day started positively.

After the second prayer, around one o'clock, when the sun was at its highest, there was the first hot meal. On Friday, after the midday prayer, they read from the Quran before they ate their lunch.

The rebels all ate in the small kitchen. I had to eat by myself. I put my sleeping bag to one side and then used my bed as a table. When it was solid food, the guard passed it through the hatch. The

43

hatch was too small to move the plate horizontally, so the guard gave the plate diagonally, but a bowl of soup or porridge could not pass horizontally, and they had to bring it in. "Mwa," they would say. Most of the time, they wished me *priyatnova appetita*, enjoy your meal. If they had to bring the food in, the guards said, *"Baltimor otvernis! Na menya ni smotri, ya bez maski."* That meant, "turn around! Don't look at me; I'm without a mask." I had to turn around and stand in the back of the room. Although "mwa" did not sound very friendly, I always showed my gratitude for the food. General was the only guard that stayed in my room for some chit chat. After lunch, it was usually quiet in the kitchen. They all left for the big room. Then it was time to guide me to the bathroom for my first daily wash.

The guards held the third prayer when the shadow began to stretch again. The fourth prayer was just after sunset when it was dusk. After the prayer, the second hot meal followed.

Povar was not a bad cook, and he prepared simple, healthy, and varied meals. His menu included cooked spaghetti with strips of beef. His pasta sauce contained tomatoes, onion, and carrots. Also, Povar liked to cook cabbage soup with boiled meat, carrots, onions, and potatoes. He cooked other favorites such as kidney bean soup, boiled, peeled potatoes, and baked potatoes. Also, there was almost always meat. There was plenty of bread and tea. They said I got the same food as they did.

When I walked through the kitchen to the bathroom, I saw the same food on their plates. After dinner, the rebels sat together in the kitchen for a while. General read and talked a bit. I could not understand the stories and conversations. They spoke in their native Caucasian language amongst themselves.

When it was completely dark, the fifth prayer followed. Just before or after the fifth prayer, I could leave for my second daily wash. The fighters went to bed early, probably because they had to get up first thing in the morning to start the prayer schedule again. There was no electricity, but soon they would fix their generator. Then they could watch TV.

General: "If you behave properly, you can also take a look now and then."

I did not know what the guys did during the daytime. Between meals and their washing rituals, it was quiet in and around the kitchen. It did not interest me that much either as long as they left me alone and treated me with respect. There was always one guard in the area that kept an eye on me, guided me to the toilet, or gave me water if needed.

The guards got tired of guiding me to the toilet several times per day. I got two plastic bottles. One for drinking water that I could fill when I went to the bathroom and one to urinate. That one I emptied when I went outside for my "big need."

Kavkazki Krest: "Don't you drink Kvass?"

Me: "No, do you want some?"

But he did not want the liquid from my bottle even though the liquid looked like the yellowish Russian soft drink made from fermented rye bread. Vendors sold the soft drink in the summer on every street corner from large tanks.

Me: Do you celebrate September 11?

I was a little worried. The rebels might have wanted to behead me. It was, after all, the first anniversary of this memorable event for Muslim fanatics.

General: "No. We are proud of Bin Laden that he went to fight against the USA. But we disapprove of killing innocent civilians, let alone celebrating it."

In the middle of the night, they banged on my door. I woke up and hoped for good news. The men came into the room with a large package. It was a box. Did the package have something to do with September 11th? Were they going to kill me?

It was not all that exciting. The box contained a mattress, a duvet, and a pillow. Most probably a sign that I had to stay longer than two months. Bringing me these items was a sign that General sympathized with me. He helped me make the best of the situation. He again showed his humane side.

To get through the days, I recalled my entire life in as much detail as possible, starting with my first memory. I remembered sitting on a plastic tractor in the streets of Rotterdam. The mental exercise ended with the memory of my kidnapping. I had a good and carefree life and traveled and experienced a lot. I wanted that life back.

I wondered if I could have prevented the kidnapping and if I made significant mistakes. I did not come to Dagestan unprepared. I received my briefings about the region. Part of my extended family came from Dagestan. I had a colleague abducted in Chechnya. Why did I have to challenge fate?

But now that my abduction had come to pass, I must also undergo the consequences. I knew kidnappings happened here, and I gambled and lost. We had unarmed security, a curfew, and movement restrictions. It all contributed to a safer environment. But still, the precautions did not guarantee a hundred percent safety.

I hoped DWB would get me out. I hoped they understood the culture of the kidnappers. Kidnappers did not care whether DWB was a good organization or not. The most critical issue for them was the payment of my ransom. The prompt payment was the most important for me as well.

The game we were in now had to be played by the local rules. We all entered the game without complaining, no excuse for not knowing the rules. No one could change the negotiation rules because you would lose before the end if you did change the practices of paying a ransom. The person who lost the game lost their life, my life. You cannot free someone without paying a ransom. I joined the contest by coming here, and I would have to follow the rules. My rules were "do not act aggressively" and "do not try to escape." Would DWB play by the rules, or would they play with my life?

I asked if there were any other books than the booklet about the divine miracles?

The guards had some military magazines. I never read much in Russian, but now I had no choice. They had a volume of the Russian edition of "Soldier of Fortune" and a "Military Parade" volume. The "Soldier of Fortune" magazine recounted the stories of Russian soldiers' adventures during their wars, raids, and partnerships between Russia and Russian-minded countries. Military Parade provided the latest developments within the Russian arms industry. Various manufacturers showed their latest weapons.

I never had a deep interest in the army or weapons and have not been a conscript. The articles in Military Parade did not interest me at all. To counteract the boredom, I decided to read every story, every test, and every sales pitch.

The guards taunted, "As a spy, do not you know everything about the Russian weapon industry? These are old editions. Why do you want to reread this?"

Me: "Repetition is the mother of knowledge."

Another occupation was the eradication of a population of small beetles. There were insects in the bark of the new tree trunks. Most of the beetles were three to nine millimeters (one-tenth to three tenths an inch). They came towards the candles; they walked on the ceiling and in my sleeping bag. In the beginning, I did not feel sorry to kill these small animals. As the number of dead bugs increased, I felt remorse. Like me, they also had the right to life, and I deprived them as my guards deprived me of my life. Also, my awe for God increased during the first few weeks. I sometimes thought that God had punished me for my sins. When I did not hear any news after a few weeks, I stopped the beetle killing for a few days. I hoped that God would reward me. I hoped my captors would take a photo or video of me as proof of life. It would prove to DWB that I was alive. Then DWB could pay the ransom.

After the first two weeks in my underground room, I managed to accept my situation. My routine consisted of:

- Receiving food through a hatch in the door.
- Going to the toilet with two guards behind me.
- Taking a shower with a bucket once a week.
- Staying underground.
- Not seeing other faces.

This life of incarceration was, of course, humiliating. But it was a logical consequence that resulted from my situation. The guards did not make it more difficult than it already was. They did not show any aggression or desire to humiliate me. The toilet was outside, there was no running water, and there was no electricity. There was indeed a good chance that I would try to escape if allowed to walk around free. If I saw their faces, betrayal was a possibility.

I disapproved of the situation. It was difficult, but it could have been so much worse! Besides, I still believed that it would soon be over. Only a month to go. I was already halfway.

The permanent group of guards consisted of General, Povar, Professor, and Tank. Sometimes General left for a few days but then returned. I realized that Povar was not their cook at all. Every day someone else had kitchen police duty. They rotated kitchen duty and hideout duty. A rebel cooked for everyone, looked after me and cleaned their hideout. Every security guard cooked a specialty dish. General loved white cabbage and almost always made soup, and Povar liked to make kidney bean soup. Professor and Tank wanted to make spaghetti or something with potatoes.

If General had his kitchen duty, I could sit in the kitchen for a chat while enjoying a cup of tea. For me, these were the best times in captivity. It gave me variety. I could stay out of my little cage a little longer. I had the opportunity to get to know the head guard better and to strengthen our bond. It seemed to work.

General: "I know what you're going through. I have been in a similar situation, but not as a hostage. I am glad you understand that hero behavior can only harm you."

Me: "Is there any news about how long it will take?"

General: "No, unfortunately not; I don't want to give you false hope."

Rebels always greeted each other with "Salaam Aleikum, W'aleikum asalaam." I asked if the greeting once per day was not enough? In answer to my question, General told me that good Muslims should greet each other whenever they enter a room. They encouraged me to say their salutation in Arabic. I had not done so because of my dissatisfaction with their religion.

Kavkazki Krest did not come that often, but he came to my room every time he was there.

Kavkazki Krest: "Baltimor, how are you? Another month and then you will be home again."

Me: "Really?"

Kavkazki Krest: "Yes, I spoke to someone again, and he told me that the negotiations are going well. DWB wants to pay, so that will be fine."

Me: "Another month, but why doesn't General say anything?"

Kavkazki Krest: "Did General tell you when he's coming back? Everything else good, how do the

51

boys behave, do they stay away from you? Do you still think a bit about the females? Do not do dirty things here in your room. Are you still pushing yourself up? Also, make knee bends; otherwise, you can no longer walk properly. Who knows, we might have to cross the mountains once we drop you off in Georgia, for example. That is a three-day walk. I've done it before."

Me: "Are you staying long?"

Kavkazki Krest: "No General will be back tomorrow. I'll come and say goodbye to you."

They were only small chats about nothing, but they brightened my attitude. Kavkazki Krest did not have to talk to me.

It was late September when the door opened unexpectedly. There was never any contact in the evening. Three of the guards were in front of me in full combat gear.

General: "Arjan, we will blindfold you and handcuff you, and then we will go outside. It is to make you feel better."

General did not sound friendly, and I felt the end of my life approaching. Did DWB abandon me? Betrayed and defeated, I felt weakness in my knees as though I would collapse.

Chapter 5
For Good Behavior

General: "Davai na progulku, eto dlya tebya. Come on; you need to go for a walk. It is good for you. Starting today, we go for a walk every day."

They put on the blindfold and handcuffs, something they did not do since my first toilet session. I accepted the situation and trusted General. We walked past the toilet. The handcuffs do not work well, and I already had one hand free.

General: "Because you have behaved so well, I have decided to let you out for half an hour every evening."

I could walk back and forth on a small piece of grass. General told me that I should also do some stretching exercises. I saw two rebels watching me. They were a bit tense and kept their kalashnikovs ready. When I walked back and forth, I saw a small red light in the bushes. A third guard watched me from behind a tree.

The airing was fantastic. It was good for me to be outside, to breathe in the fresh air. Finally, I could fully stretch, jump, and walk without getting dizzy and nauseous.

The next day they only handcuffed me. When I showed General that I freed my hands right away, he did not bother to cuff me anymore. After a while, only two guards joined me. I pretended that I did not see the weapons to feel free. Sometimes it worked. Sometimes Povar pointed his gun at me. With a Kalashnikov, it was scarier.

Every day two different guards brought me outside. It also allowed me to get to know the men a little better. We slowly but surely started to have real conversations about religion and politics. I had a good knowledge of the Bible that was useful, just like my basic knowledge of Islam. Strict believers respect believers more than total unbelievers. Muslims could not understand that people believe nothing at all. They saw that as a kind of mental emptiness.

They saw me as a representative of all the evil from the Western culture. They distinguished no difference between the USA and Europe. I tried to convince them that there was a difference. These fundamentalists hated Jews. They thought the Jewish state was after world domination. In their minds, it was the Jews who flew two Boeings into the Twin Towers. It was the Jews that set the Americans against Muslims.

For them, the West was a cesspool of sin. All Western women were prostitutes. In Western culture, homosexuals could marry. In contrast,

Muslims preferred to kill them. I tried to teach them something about our society and that life was not so black and white.

To increase my knowledge about Islam, I read the book "Divine Miracles." I wanted to contribute to religious discussions. "Divine Miracles" attempted to convince the reader of the existence of God. The miracles described should make people cross the threshold to Islam.

My guards took the miracles described in the book seriously, but they did not need the miracles for themselves. They were already firmly convinced. The miracles were needed to convince the unbelievers. They were pleased that in present-day life, God showed His presence through miracles.

Not long after they started to let me out for evening walks, they hooked up the generator. The guards could watch television in the evening. I hoped General kept his promise to invite me to watch TV. He did after a few days. All rebels watched TV from their beds with the Kalashnikovs within reach. I sat against the wall.

"Salaam alaikum," I said. Some looked surprised, and some said something back. One of the rebels flipped to the public channel in Dagestan. Quickly General told him to change the channel. I guess General did not want me to know that we were in Dagestan instead of Chechnya.

General: "If the Russian army gets close and we can't escape, then I have to shoot you. I will not let you fall into the hands of the police or the army alive. I do not want to lose my Chechen's honor, so we will first try to escape. We have good surveillance here to warn us, and we will take you with us. I tell you this because we have information that the Russians will come here tonight. We really might have to leave."

Back in my room, I was tense. I hoped and prayed that the Russians were not coming because I would not survive. The warriors would not drag me along for too long.

General: "Arjan, we just got a call, Professor and I are going to have a look. We may have to flee tonight. Just go and watch television with Tank and Povar. We will try to get you out alive."

I did not want to watch television. How could I watch TV with all the uncertainty? The possibility of fleeing made my heart beat hard and fast. I felt nervous. Why did this have to happen before my imminent release in mid-October?

Tank and Povar came to get me to watch television. Their troubled and nervous behavior did not reassure me. Tank walked back and forth more than usual. I asked to go back to my room. Tank said, "It will be okay."

In my room, I was too nervous to rest by lying on top of my bed. I positioned myself at the end of the bed close to the door. My legs were going back and forth. For the second time since my arrival, I felt terrified!

Halfway through the night, I heard, "Allahu Akbar, Allahu akbar." It was the first time I enjoyed hearing them call upon Allah. Professor and Tank returned from reconnaissance.

They reported, "The Russians are not coming. Of course, they do not dare go into hostile territory at night, cowards." I went to bed, relieved.

Fifteen October was close, and there was still no news. I doubted my release. General also seemed gloomy.

Life in captivity was getting better. I enjoyed airing and occasional television. The diversions helped, but I was bored as hell. The uncertainty gave me stress.

Amina's birthday on September 22nd passed. In my thoughts, I spent her birthday with her. I decided to celebrate every birthday of somebody close to me like that.

I spent hours figuring out what would be the safest way to hand over my ransom. I sat in the corridor when General was cooking. I explained my half-baked plans to him. I proposed to negotiate my release on my behalf. He said he had faith in his negotiators.

All in all, I am alone in the dark for 23 hours a day. I tried to read through the magazines as much as possible. After six weeks, I could not reread the same magazine. I asked General to buy some books for me.

The crime series called "Brigada" gave me some variety in my life. The guards were fans of the series. They enthusiastically discussed the plot twists. It was such a highlight that I did not mind staying here to watch the series' end.

We ate much better than the average Dagestani family because we had luxury products such as mayonnaise, ketchup, and lots of meat. An average Dagestani family grows their vegetables. I was not only looking forward to groceries and yogurt but also news from the outside world.

With little hope for a release, I counted down my last washing day on Saturday, 12 October. Every Saturday, I showered and washed my clothes with a bucket of water. Not only did I count the days, but also the number of humiliating visits to "Putin." I walked into the laundry room and saw General's gun in his holster. He forgot his Beretta and extra cartridges.

I was almost free. I just had to shoot Professor and General, and I was out. The first one would be Professor and then the others. I would run down the mountains, stop a car, and promise the driver 10,000 dollars. I was so happy to be home soon.

I opened the door, and Professor looked up. I saw his big eyes through the cracks in the mask. "Take it away," I said while pointing to the belt in the bathroom. Professor came carefully closer and removed the belt. I closed the door and washed. In those few seconds, I decided to return the gun. I could have shot Professor or held him hostage. There were two more guards inside and one outside. The chance had been small that I could have killed them all. Did I want to live with the heaviness of four lives on my soul? Did I act like a coward, or was it an intelligent move? I guess it is better this way. My release would happen soon.

While we watched TV, General said nothing about the incident with his gun.

Me: "Didn't you notice that your gun was still in the bathroom?"

General: "It was just for testing; there were no bullets in it. Professor should have looked in the bathroom before you went in."

Me: "As you can see now, you can trust me. I could have shot Professor and everyone else."

General: "You could not have succeeded, and you would be dead now."

Me: "You know I can't get used to guards who are so close to me when using the toilet. Can they stand a little further away?"

General: "I'll consider it. I guess you want to go to your room now."

15 October passed with disappointment. Against all odds, I believed it would only take two months. How long would I have to sit here? The emptiness of existence was almost unbearable. I lived 90% of my time locked up in a small, dark room with beetles. I had nothing to stimulate my mind. I had no pen, paper, books, no sunlight, no music, no friends, no family, not even faces. What I had was armed rebels in camouflage and a bottle for my pee. Before doing something, I had to ask for permission. Remaining in a constant state of alert was exhausting. It seemed my energy had run out.

What was DWB doing? Did they want to pay? Did they understand for my release to come to fruition, they needed to pay a ransom? Maybe the kidnappers had not made contact yet.

I had a few difficult days. I tried to stay positive, but it did not always work. I thought about worse situations: a dark cellar with only water and bread to eat, a kick in the face every morning, or an occasional body part cut off to put more pressure on the paying party.

November 3 was my oldest brother Edger's birthday. My release would be a nice gift for him. I tried to cheer myself up a bit by suggesting that I call him from Moscow.

General asked me to sing Dutch songs during a television evening. I liked music but had a hard time with the lyrics. I remembered from long ago Oerend Hard, the first hit of Normaal. General tried to sing "Uhu" with me. General sang battle songs in return. It was a strange situation.

As usual, I woke up around eleven in the morning. I heard helicopters flying over the hideout, and within an hour, I had counted five helicopters. Strangely enough, I did not hear any noise from the rebels. No call to pray and no sounds from the kitchen, either. Around lunchtime, General gave me some bread and explained that I could not go to the outside toilet. He ordered me to put on my shoes. This order was strange because house rules did not permit the wearing of shoes inside the hideout.

General: "Be quiet; there are Russians in the neighborhood, awfully close. We cannot flee anymore. If they discover us, we will probably all die. We will not surrender; if we die, we will die as martyrs and go directly to heaven."

I was nervous, and I felt my heart pounding again. I walked to the plastic vent pipe in the corner to listen. I heard the rebels whisper and people shouting outside. I sat silently with my arms crossed on the bed and listened intently. The screams were subsiding. For a moment, it was utterly silent. Then the rebels came inside and mumbled Allahu Akbar. I took a breath of relief and whispered Allahu Akbar as well. God had protected me, as well.

General: "They will tell the commander that they entered all the houses. They always scream because they are scared. Muslim rebels are not afraid of dying. They have Allah, who protects them or calls them to heaven. Russian soldiers are scared and drink vodka to drink away the fear. That's why they make so much noise."

General left the last weekend in October. He would return with Ramadan in early November. Before he left, he asked me for the phone number and address of my parents.

Me: "You already have contact with my side; why do you need these phone numbers now?"

General: "Just give them now. If it helps you get free, why not?"

Without an end date, it became increasingly difficult to remain positive. My brother's birthday was in a few days, and I chose December 5 as a new release date. I had finished 75 days, only 35 more days to December 5. This year, Ramadan and the Dutch Santa Claus coincided. Who knows, it might be one big party.

Things were not getting any better in my room. There were all kinds of woodworms in the tree trunks. Wood pulp started to fall from the ceiling. In the beginning, I could avoid it. But now there was no escape. The sawdust fell on me non-stop.

A rebel solved the wood pulp rain by putting a sheet against the ceiling. Povar ruined my improved mood. I still had a problematic relationship with him. I told him he behaved like John Wayne, the actor. Povar had a cavalier habit of pointing his gun at me. He did not know who John Wayne was. After my explanation, he felt honored. He did not get my hint and still pointed his gun at me. So, we sometimes clashed.

Povar: "Baltimor, hurry up; how long can you brush your teeth."

I forgot my 'toilet' bottle because of the hurry, so I knocked on the door and asked Povar to get it for me.

Povar: "Baltimor, you always leave something lying around. I am not your walking dog. Just relax; you'll get your bottle tomorrow!"

After ten minutes, Professor brought me the bottle. Povar yelled at Professor for standing up for me. I appreciated Professor taking my side.

Ramadan was close at hand. How hard was it to fast a month?

Chapter 6
Ramadan

It was the first time that I participated in Ramadan. Somehow, I was looking forward to it. People in the Muslim religion knew Ramadan as a time of reflection and peace. Fasting could help cure my intestinal problems.

At first, I refused to join them until they said it would be easier if they did not have to prepare lunch for me while they were fasting. So to help the Muslim rebels a bit, I decided to join Ramadan. I just wanted them to know I would not convert to Islam.

The guards told me that they would devote themselves to praying and reading the Quran. The more they prayed and read from the Quran, the more Allah would reward them. During Ramadan, there was a more generous reward system than during the other months. Allah valued praying and scripture reading during Ramadan more. The rebels were not sure how big the multiplier was.

My knowledge about their interpretation of Islam was growing every day. Muslim extremism was a hot topic. I imagined what it would be like to do anthropological research about Muslim rebels. I was not a fully participating observer, but I learned something about their way of life. I could return after my release as a guest.

Due to the lack of water, it was difficult to shave. The rebels were excited about my full beard. Mustaches were cut short. To strengthen my position, I had left my beard since mid-October. I warned myself not to lose my mental freedom.

Allah did not like people to have evil thoughts. Allah punished people for uttering their bad ideas. Allah gave rewards to people that kept evil thoughts inside. Thus, remaining silent was gold. Praying to Allah only counts when the words passed your lips. At least you had to murmur the prayer. Praying out loud on the toilet or in unclean places was forbidden.

Using water sparingly was important. My fellow participants in Ramadan grumbled at me because I used too much water. The prophet Muhammad said that even when you washed on a riverbank, you still had to use water sparingly. The stones on which you stood may not get wet. In the house where we were, the greatest threats to losing your cleanliness were doing needs. If you broke the cleanliness, you must wash again. You lost cleanliness by touching the private area and the inside of the thighs. There were no women in the area and no unclean food, so we had less cause to become dirty.

Povar suffered from flatulence, which occasionally caused some comical situations. During the airing, he relieved the flatulence. He had to clean five times a day most of the time. You could not pray to Allah with dirty clothing.

Leftovers were not thrown away but eaten. General expected me to eat all the food off my plate with a bread crust. I thought it had something to do with their religion. General explained to me that this saved water when cleaning the dishes.

Since I was in their midst, the lack of trust had been one of the biggest problems. I did not trust my situation would end well. They thought of me as a spy, maybe a Jew. Of course, I was curious. I wanted to learn as much as possible. It was challenging to ask everything directly. Asking too much instantly increased their suspicion. If I knew too much, there was more danger for them after my release.

Sometimes I thought their piety was for show. But why would my devout Muslim rebels do that? They did not:

- Smoke tobacco or drugs.
- Drink alcoholic beverages.
- Swear.
- Allow women in the house.
- Watch scantily dressed women or worse on TV.

They prayed plenty of times, read religious books, and their behavior towards me was not aggressive. Why would they put on a show?

I had learned that Allah allowed Muslims to lie in two cases. Married people with relationship problems could lie to save or improve the relationship. In the Jihad, the fight to spread Islam, lying was allowed.

I had not been able to catch General in a lie. He had kept all his promises. His firm beliefs gave me a framework that helped me increase my trust in him.

General brought me a new mattress when he returned. The old one started to mold because of the high humidity in my underground room. I decided to put the bed straight up during the day so that it could air out. I took the mattress as a bad sign. Books would have been better than a new mattress.

General: "Arjan, the process started again. A new intermediary had been appointed to conduct the negotiations. The first one did not meet the qualifications. That was why we needed the telephone numbers of your family. An intermediary must be someone with a lot of influence and power and not disturbed by the police or security services. It is often someone who works within the police, politics, or security services. The intermediary is regarded highly and is untouchable. Yet it remains difficult because there are always people who act as jammers.   DWB is, of course, also closely monitored."

Ramadan promised to be a productive month. Early in the morning, the rebel on duty knocked on the door. I dressed quickly and ate something. Then I went back to bed and continued to sleep until the afternoon prayer. The days were even more similar than before. We ate before dawn and just after sunset and fasted during the day. This daily schedule gave a welcome regularity.

After a long wait, the rebels finally bought books for me. It was the best thing that happened to me. Together there were around 1200 pages. I intended to read only 40 pages each day. Before reading the new 40 pages, I planned to read the pages I had already read. So, I could enjoy the three books for two months.

General gave me more attention, and I spent more time in the kitchen than before. I regarded his presence as protective.   The guards did not misbehave when he was not there, but they removed some flexibility from my life.

In the Soviet Union, Russians knew Caucasians as hot-tempered.   I noticed that Povar and Tank were somewhat impatient. They quickly lost their temper. Several rebels said that their conversion to Islam had calmed them down. They tried to adhere to the prescribed religious rules. They had the goal of going to heaven after death. They admitted that it was not always easy. According to them, Satan still lurked to get people off the right track. Life on earth was just an intermediate station. They accepted the sober life. They preferred an eternal good life over a good experience on earth. It became clear to me that their level of knowledge varied.

They tried to stimulate each other to learn Arabic to understand the Quran better. They discussed various interpretations of the Quran. They read texts and verses to each other.

After conversations with the guards, I understood the appeal faith had for these men. It gave their lives a higher purpose in a world that still seemed hostile to them. In the North Caucasus, many people see Russia as a ruler. In Chechnya, the lives of young men were made exceedingly difficult by the Russian army.

General: "Young men are arrested, abused, and sometimes disappear. Their family never sees them again. Try to imagine it. An interrogator pushes a plastic pipe with a piece of barbed wire into their anus. Then the interrogator removes the piece of pipe out so that the barbed wire remains. Then the barbed wire is pulled out all at once. Every family has someone who was killed or abused. Do you find it strange that we fight against the Russians?"

Russia discriminated against Chechens and other Caucasian nationalities. Because of their darker complexions, they were easy to distinguish from Russians. Chechens wanted control of their land and destiny. Separation from Russia would put an end to the brutality.

Professor: "Imagine an Islamic state. There is no alcohol, drugs, and smoking addiction. There is no prostitution or discrimination. We could use all the money spent on addictions and decadence on the poor. The money saved can be spent to educate the people and build infrastructure."

Faith gave them strength, peace, and hope for a better life. There was also brotherhood; people stood up for each other. They supported each other in good and bad times. There was a hierarchy to take care of the needs of family members and subordinates.

As a child, my parents taught me Christianity, but we did not have strict religious training. After we were old enough to decide for ourselves, we no longer had to go to church against our will. We attended church for Easter, Christmas, weddings, and funerals. At Protestant Christian primary and secondary school, I did take religious lessons where the teachers shared the stories from the Bible in an exciting way. Because of this Christian training, I have remembered many accounts from the Bible.

I had never been deeply religious. Although I had some idea that there might be a God somewhere, I never let this feeling lead my life.

My way of thinking was that people were responsible for their actions. We have many choices.

But we do not control the options that come to us. As a result, we have less influence on life than we think. Also, the supply of choices depends on the physical and mental environment in which we live.

God may provide us with choices. But the options we have maybe random or coincidence. There may be no cohesion at all. Is it essential to know?

In captivity, I was more concerned about fundamental questions than in freedom. The spiritual environment was contagious. I thought more about religion. Religious thought gave me more opportunities to engage in conversations with the guards.

Who knows if there was a God? Could God help me? Or was that hypocrisy comparable to wartime when people attended the churches?

In recent years I had called on Him, but not like now. It was never too late to let God into my heart. Perhaps my situation was a sign from God to make me realize that it was not too late.

Some guards said, "Perhaps Allah wants you to know more about Islam, and that is why you are sitting here." According to them, not everyone could find a way to God.

My captivity meant death was closer to me now. I preferred to go to heaven instead of hell. In my many hours of boredom, I considered all my sins. I used the Ten Commandments as my guide.

Unfortunately, I only knew seven of them. I asked forgiveness for the sins I regretted. I also intended not to commit those sins anymore. I consistently tried to pray in the evenings and in the morning.

Yet even now, during Ramadan, I was unable to hold on to my beliefs. The sense of hypocrisy overcame me, and I stopped praying.

Occasionally I prayed for news but did not receive an answer. I liked fasting, and I wanted to complete the month. The guards did not understand why I joined them. Fasting gave me regularity. It seemed to be good for my health.

Muslims are not allowed to maintain friendships with non-believers. Yet mutual respect developed between General and me. General got along best with Professor. The pillar of their camaraderie was religion. Professor was becoming more friendly and seemed to trust me more than before. While we were airing, we always had something to discuss. Professor invited me, just like General, to come and sit in the kitchen while he cooked.

Me: "Why do you keep buying yogurt and Aquafresh for me?"

Professor: "We are depriving you of your freedom. We take almost everything away from you. By giving you the yogurt and toothpaste that you used in freedom, we try to give you back something of your own life."

Now that I had books, I realized how great the boredom used to be. I could not imagine how I got through those two months. Reading in Russian was not too bad, especially after the second reading. I understood the common thread, although about 30 percent of the words remained unclear.

As I approached the end of the book, the fear of loneliness and boredom came over me. The reading got slower and slower. The moment I read the last words, I cried. I was so afraid of future boredom that it made me panic.

Unfortunately, there was still time left to get bored. I walked back and forth a lot. I tried to keep myself moving as much as possible. I felt the temptation to lie in bed a lot but intended not to do so. I did some push-ups. I did not want to sweat too much because there was not much opportunity to wash. I also realized that it was useless to aim for a fit body. The imminency of death and burial 6 feet under the ground undermined my goal of a healthy and robust body.

When Povar or Tank had the cooking duty, they never invited me. When General or Professor had kitchen duty, I had the chance to get an invitation to sit in the kitchen. I understood that it was difficult for them. The rebels could not walk back and forth without worry. They had to wear a mask and watch the knives.

With the airing and the visits to the kitchen, contact with General became more frequent. We got to know each other little by little. Confidence increased slightly, but mutual suspicion still existed. He said he had a good education. By the skillful way he interacted with me and his men, he could have received an education as a teacher.

One of the films I often have to think about is the Papillon film with Steve McQueen as a French prisoner. When I asked General how I looked, he always answered: "You look good, like Steve McQueen." Although Steve McQueen looked far from good after years of isolation. Because General had seen many films, it was a fun and neutral topic of discussion. Besides movies, I talked to him about politics, women, and religion.

I explained to him what DWB was doing in Chechnya and Dagestan. I thought it strange that the rebels were abducting humanitarian aid workers.

I visited Chechnya several times before my abduction. I met a lot of Chechen people in those four months. I did not find many Chechens religious. They wanted their country to become independent of Russia, but most did not want an Islamic state. Chechens had dark memories of the Islamic state after the first war with Russia. That was a time of violence and lawlessness.

Me: "Is it smart to pursue an Islamic state? Chechens want separation from Russia, but they are not religious."

General: "Ordinary civilians are tired of fighting. When rebels arrive in their village, they support us. If the Russians are there, they support the Russians."

General was probably not contradicted much, but now and then I did. I explained that people in the Netherlands did not like authoritarian behavior.

General and I disagreed about how to roast the meat. We contended over the amount of salt in the rice, sauce, or spaghetti. I tried to restrain myself. But when I could no longer bear his cooking style, I refused to follow his instructions. His mood changed.

Me: "You certainly can't handle it if someone contradicts you."

General: "Yes, I am the commander here, and I should be listened to."

Me: "I am your prisoner, but I am not part of your group, so you are not my commander."

I felt his anger but could not see it because of the mask.

General: "It is not the place to be stubborn here."

Me: "I got that from my mother. She often pretends to be listening, but still does her things."

General: "Did you learn to cook from your mother?"

Me: "There are things that I learned from her."

General: "If your mother says so, then it's okay."

General's parents had already died, but he still spoke of them with lots of love.

While cooking, General also started saying "thank you" and "please" for the first time. It felt like a small victory.

The rebels kept quiet in the winter and made it difficult for the Russians in the summer. There were also sad stories about Russian cruelty done to some of the rebels' family members. Hatred for the Russians was everywhere. The exiled Chechen president Maschadov was the official president for them.

There were enough indicators that I was not in Chechnya. It was hard to believe that all the guards were Chechens. Maybe a few of them were, but I had reasons to think most of them were Dagestani.

I doubted their Chechen origin since my arrival. In my opinion, it was not possible to drive through Chechnya in the dark because of the curfew. During the airing, I heard cars traveling at night.

The language they spoke did not resemble Chechen. There were too many throaty sounds that did not occur in Chechen. I also saw a dictionary in the kitchen that was not Chechen-Russian.

Povar once told me by accident that we were in Dagestan. General did not want me to watch the Dagestani channel. I thought they spoke a bit too much about Chechnya. Their Chechen war stories lacked details. It sounded a bit like wannabee Chechens. I also noticed that Povar and Professor, for example, played a lot with their weapons. Was this because they missed battle, or was it because they had not experienced combat yet?

On the last Saturday of November, we almost finished Ramadan. We had wash day on Saturday, and I washed my clothes and bedding in a large red tub first. Then I got water to clean myself. I had one pair of boxer shorts and one T-shirt, which I wore all week. I also had two pairs of socks that I rarely wore, a tracksuit and another pair of jeans. Hand washing was a necessary evil.

It was getting colder outside, so the laundry hardly dried. Oil lamps had recently replaced the candles in the house. I pressed the wet clothes against the warm glass of my oil lamp to speed up the drying process.

General came in the late afternoon and happily knocked on my door.

General: "Arjan life is full of good surprises. I have good news. During the airing tonight, I will tell you."

I felt energized and could hardly wait. Rumor had it that I could go home before the end of Ramadan. Ramadan concluded next Thursday. Will December 5 be the big day?

Chapter 7
Below Zero

A white blanket of snow covered the world at the start of the meteorological winter. Slowly but surely, the temperature fell. The dry sultry autumn we had experienced gave way to a cold winter. I had received white woolen socks and long male underwear named Anita and made in Iran. My cold-weather wardrobe consisted of long underwear, an old green sweater, and a plastic jacket. In one of the military magazines, I read that you stayed warmer without clothes in bed than with clothes. It was already below zero Celsius outside at night and about the same inside. We had no heater, and the front door was open during the day. Soon the temperature dropped so low that I needed an extra sleeping bag. I slept with "Anita," and that was nice. I had to hold on a while longer, and then I could go home!

We celebrated Ramadan's end with all kinds of sweets, including cake, fruit, and delicious cookies. I achieved one of Islam's five pillars to the delight of the Muslim rebels. Maybe they thought I would convert to a Muslim. Fasting improved my intestinal problem, and I intended to stick to Ramadan again next year at home for health reasons. At this time in the year, my family usually celebrates Sinterklaas, Dutch Santaclaus. Would they skip a year like I had to? I had no idea how my family was doing. They must think of me a lot and had terrible imaginations about how I was doing. If only they knew how my life would be here, it would give them some ease.

In the last few days, I felt miserable. Ramadan had concluded ten days ago. My release did not come to pass yet. Due to a lack of news, the uncertainty was increasing. It was deathly cold inside, with temperatures just above zero. The wood started to mold.

General cooked more and more dishes with white cabbage and garlic. He once heard that the combination of garlic and cabbage was an anecdote for TB. For me, it deteriorated my digestive system.

I still hoped to celebrate Christmas with my family and not alone in my small room.

I reacted emotionally to all kinds of small events around me. It did not take much to make me cry. Whether Poval caused feelings of sadness triggered by little time in the laundry room, or an unexpected kind word from Professor, I still did not want the rebels to see weakness. I did not want to lose their respect.

It seemed like there was no way out, and I felt death approaching. The airing was the time for serious conversations. We took turns putting on our shoes in the hall. We went quietly outside and waited for each other at the front of the door. Then we trudged quietly in a row past the toilet to the field. We plodded along in a single file with one armed guard in the front of the line, me in the middle, and another guard behind me. We stood in the field and walked back and forth under a mostly clear sky with visible stars and moon. I enjoyed gazing at the moon and stars. The celestial bodies gave me a sense of grandeur and a sense of freedom. We tried to see the satellites that circle in their orbit around our planet.

Me: "General, do you still believe in a quick-release?"

General: "Daaah, hard to say."

"Daaah" was a longer word for the Russian "da" in the group. "Daaah" became one expression for most thoughtful states of mind.

Me: "If you have to kill me, can you put my corpse along the side of the road so that my parents know that I have died?"

I did not look at him and felt my tears burn. I walked around with this question on my mind for a while. I finally managed to ask them and felt a sense of relief.

General: "Daaah, daaah, you have managed to choose a heavy topic. Do you sit all day in your room thinking about this? You must be in a good mood! Arjan, we do not want to kill you. We just want to make some money. I will certainly try to get you back home alive. If you get yourself killed, it is difficult to drag your corpse. So, I can't promise you that."

Me: "Then promise that you will inform my parents in one way or another."

General: "I will see what I can do."

With a slightly more reassured heart, I paced like a polar bear across the grass.

I read a lot but could not help thinking about my awkward situation. I reached my saturation point with all their commanding. The constant repeating of the commands irritated me. They treated me like a child with a short memory!

To explain the situation, I started a game of "who am I" with Tank and Povar. I imitated someone's command, and they had to guess whose it was. I began by imitating Povar.

"Turn around! Don't look at me; I don't have a mask on!"

They knew right away.

"Just look down!"

Tank repeated this again and again as he led me to the toilet.

Tank was right, and Povar did not know.

"Without knocking on the door, don't come out of the bathroom!"

Professor did not command. But he always ordered me to knock on the door before I left the bathroom so that he could put his mask back on. Professor liked to look at himself in the mirror. In the evening, he brushed his teeth at the same time as I did.

Tank and Povar knew that it came from Professor, and they laughed a bit.

"Popozhe" was immediately recognized by both. Popozhe was Tank's answer to my request to go to the toilet.

Another one of Tank's statements, "A step to the left or a step to the right is an attempt to flee, and we will shoot you!"

"Baltimor, zhivoi? Are you still alive?" When Rebel without name1 asked if I was still alive. This statement was not a command but a form of attention that I appreciated.

When the hatch in the door got jammed, they commanded, "Baltimor otkroi!" And I had to push the door open from the inside.

Tank: "Seriously, are we commanding too much?"

Me: "Yes, maybe you don't realize it. You also see that I am a normal guy just like you. By now, I especially understand how things work here."

I hoped my examples would change their behavior.

Early on, my kidnappers asked which sports I enjoyed. I told them I played soccer and golfed. Also, I mentioned that boxing and taekwondo were favorite sports. The kidnappers exaggerated my boxing prowess while handing me over to the rebel group. I did not mind because I thought it would improve my status.

During our evening walks, we often talked about boxing. Tank held up Mike Tyson as a great example of a boxer. One evening I imitated the announcement of a world title fight. "Get ready to rumble! Fighting out of the blue corner, introducing the challenger, he stands 6 feet 5 inches tall, weighing in at 255 pounds. He holds a professional boxing record of 37 wins and 4 losses, with 13 wins by knockout. He is fighting out of London, England: "Bone Crusher" Smith! Fighting out of the red corner, introducing the World Super Heavyweight Champion, he stands at 6 feet 4 inches tall, weighing in at 260 pounds. He holds a professional boxing record of 30 wins and 0 losses, 28 by knockout. He is fighting out of Grozny, Chechnya: Aslanbek the Lion!" The guards did not understand English, but they were impressed with my performance.

General had been challenging me for a while to spar with him. In the kitchen, we had played around. I felt it was in the best interest of our relationship not to spar with General.

During television time, the guards wrestled. Even though I lacked wrestling skills, General and I wrestled outside a few times, and I lost 4 out of 5 matches.

One of the rebels asked, "Are you such a bad wrestler, or do you pretend to be weaker than you are."

I replied, "I can easily beat General. If I had won, I would have to become your leader. I do not want to do that to him"

General continued to challenge me, and it worried me. There was no upside for me to spar with General. Either the men would lose respect for me or respect for General. Both hypotheticals result in dire outcomes for me. Frankly, I did not want to get beat up. I had seen that General had some martial arts experience.

In my room, I hoped that there was no boxing that night. In the evening, General indeed did not come to air me. I think he wanted the bluffing to come to an end. The other guards were already a little excited about our so-called fight.

The day after, I said something about him not showing up. He replied that he thought I was smarter than mentioning it! Tonight was boxing time.

Kavkazki Krest watched while we behaved like roosters. Even with thin leather gloves, I did not dare strike him with full force. He did not punch hard at first either, but then he became more excited. I lost my balance when I missed him. He immediately gave me another jab above my eye. Then I changed strategy. I drove him into the bushes and hit him on his left eye. At that point, we both understood that it was better to stop.

In the evening, when I washed, I saw my black eye. A bit later, General came to my room. He wanted to see how I was doing. He told me, "I got you. You are the one with a black eye." He laughed a bit. Then he pushed his mask a bit aside and showed me that he also had a black eye. I appreciated the gesture. He could have pretended that I did not hit him.

Today there was no lunch. It was deathly quiet in and around the house. Must I remain silent or knock on the door. The guards did not warn me to be silent. But still, Russian soldiers could find me and shoot me by mistake. I had a large red beard like many Chechens.

General eased my mind and put me in the kitchen.

General: "There are problems again; the Russians are nearby."

Me: I heard some gunshots in the distance.

General: "I have forbidden my men to shoot them. If they do not see us, we are safe. If we shoot them, more Russians will come tomorrow, and we may be in a lost situation."

Although the situation was tense, I could stay in the kitchen. General did not seem nervous and continued to peel the potatoes. Later, bad news arrived.

General: "Two of our brothers were shot about 40 kilometers from here in a firefight with the Russians. I have sent Tank and Povar to them."

Me: "Do I know your brothers?"

General, "No, they are brothers but not from our group."

Me: "Aren't you sad?"

General: "Yes, but luckily they have died as "shahidi," martyrs, and end up in heaven right away."

I heard Professor return in the evening alone. In the morning, I noticed that General and Professor were the only two attending the morning prayer. I did not feel comfortable. Did the Russians kill or capture Povar and Tank? Would the Russians be here soon?

Povar returned. Tank suffered a severe head injury and may never return. Tank had often said that he would like to die as a martyr. General told me that it would have been better for Tank if he had died.

All of Tank's family died in the war with the Russians, including his wife. He had a quiet and reflective demeanor. Tank had journeyed through

Russia and Czechoslovakia and enjoyed talking about his travels.

He was a bit rude and stiff. Sometimes he showed his soft side by quoting a supportive verse from the Quran when he thought I felt distressed by my incarceration.

Tank: "I guess you want to cry now and then? I do. It helps a bit, but then you have to continue."

Other rebels read a lot from the Quran; he just read through it and spent more time with his dictionary. He encouraged me to fast. He had also read a book by a Canadian who recommended fasting.

As far as I could judge it, he did not have anything against me. But on the other side, he did not do much to make it easier for me.

I endured Christmas in captivity, and I felt like the loneliest person. I sang Christmas songs as I walked back and forth. I would love to go to a Christmas service. I remembered the excellent food, the atmosphere at home with all the children visiting mum and dad. The food here was not bad. I knew these Muslims did not celebrate Christmas. Perhaps they have thought of me and bought something special. I soon discovered that was not the case.

Rebelname2 ordered, "Baltimor, turn around; I don't wear a mask." I hated it when he called me Baltimor. We did not have a good rapport, and I got annoyed when he called me by my nickname.

He said, "Here is a big piece of meat. Enjoy your meal."

I found a piece of meat just boiled in a large pan with water on my aluminum soup plate. The portion of meat consisted mostly of transparent fat with lots of bones and tendons. Christmas was far away.

After a few minutes, I picked up myself again. As it was often the case, I reminded myself that self-pity did not help me stay positive. Self-pity fed into my negative emotions and thoughts.

On Boxing Day, I helped General cook. It was Thursday, and they were fasting. Just before sunset, the men came into the kitchen like hungry wolves. They quickly started to eat. Today it was so cold. They were all gathering in the kitchen, where it was nice and warm. For the first time, they did not send me away. Kavkazki Krest made some jokes. Together with the rebels, I was making fun of General's cooking abilities. It was amusing to see how they were all standing in line to cleanse themselves. Of course, I knew that I was their prisoner, but now it seemed like the opposite. I was the only one without a mask, and they suffered a bit for me.

We received new snow the Saturday after Christmas, and I had always loved snow. The snow made me happy. The white world around me and the muffled sound felt reassuring. General allowed me to stay outside and enjoy the snow.

We received a letter from the outside. A new intermediary had been appointed to negotiate my release. He had transferred all the ransom requirements to DWB. The process of securing my freedom started again from scratch. It was not super good news, but I was happy that at least there was news.

One day before New Year's Eve, we stood on the lawn in the dark.

General: "Arjan, I promised to let you shoot to celebrate the new year, but I have to leave tonight. I will not be here tomorrow. If you want, you can now pull the trigger a few times."

A bit doubtful, I took the gun from him.

General: "Don't pretend you've never held a gun. We don't believe you anyway."

My first reaction was to point at Povar, but I suppressed my thoughts.

Me: "Where is the safety lock, and how do you unlock it or set it to single-shot and automatic?"

General: "You are a con artist."

Me: "No, I don't know."

They explained where the lever was, and I played a bit with the gun. It was lighter than I had imagined, and I felt adrenaline shooting through my body.

General: "If you want, I can put some bullets in it, and then you can shoot a few times in the air. We do not celebrate New Year's Eve, but we know you guys celebrate with big parties at home."

Me: "No, I do not have to celebrate New Year's Eve one day early. That makes no sense. Let me shoot the day I am released."

We agreed I would celebrate on the day of my release. I felt like I missed an opportunity of a lifetime. But drawing attention to our location was not a good idea either.

At midnight on December 31, I was already asleep. One of the many Russian superstitions was your situation would remain the same as on the last day of the year. Did I have to sit here for another year?

Chapter 8
Guard Change

The group of guards had changed. I was always with Povar and Professor. They alternated with Kavkazki Krest and Rebel without names 1 and 2.

The first weeks of the year were quiet. I did not expect any news. The new intermediary had just started. In Russia, public life came to a halt at the beginning of January. Russians celebrated the New Year holidays and Orthodox Christmas.

I renamed "Rebel without a name 1" Tajik because he cooked the Tajik dish called Plov quite well. Plov is the Central Asian variant of pilav and is one of my favorite dishes since my time in Tajikistan. Now that he was here more often, we got to know each other better. He still occasionally asked in his way if I was still alive. He climbed a step higher in my hierarchy.

Kavkazki Krest was still the joker. When the boys assembled in the kitchen because of the cold, I often heard his voice above them. The whole group laughed out loud at his jokes. Krest brightened up the entire group.

Krest never made me feel like a prisoner. Now and then, he came to my room and made some fun. I took his stories with a grain of salt. His beautiful fairy tales held the interest of the listener.

He had some stories about how he escaped from the hospital in Chechnya that DWB supported. He also had accounts about how he extorted small shops and wealthy people in Moscow.

I did not know why, but occasionally his colleague rebels called him Ali Baba.

During airing, Krest would say, "Just be careful, I will whistle for a moment, and there will be 40 robbers here. I will do it. Must I whistle?"

It was all about nothing, but his cheerfulness was a pleasant diversion for me. Krest was slightly shorter than me but had a much more massive and broader build. He said that he boxed in the army and worked in construction. He was extraordinarily strong. He beat two people arm wrestling at the same time. Looking at his big belly, he liked to eat and drink.

For Kavkazki Krest, too, religion had meant a significant change in his life. Just like the others, he tried to stay on the right track.

Kavkazki Krest: "I used to visit prostitutes and drink a lot. I can do without them now, but I still like a beer now and then. I get bored, leaving my previous lifestyle completely."

Occasionally he made fun of his colleagues in front of them. "Almost thirty years and still virgins, what a bunch of sad guys."

The wood in my room rots and continues to mold through the damp cold air. Because of General's absence, I spent more time in my room.

It was so cold outside that the toilet froze. The water supply became problematic, and the guards had to get the water with jerry cans. Washing my clothes and bedsheets was more difficult. I had been wearing the same outerwear for five weeks.

The guards had a gas heater in their room. They allowed me to heat up one time. Of course, I liked it very much, but my room felt even more like a freezer afterward. Since then, I have preferred to stay in my jail cell not exposed to temperature fluctuations.

Boredom struck again. The lack of the sun and severe cold made me remember a warmer time working in Sierra Leon. There was a lot of time for relaxation on the beach. I fantasized that I was enjoying the beach in the sun. I saw the Atlantic Ocean's blue water, the white beaches, and palm trees in my mind's eye. I remembered the children who insistently sold roasted peanuts. Also, I entertained thoughts of beautiful women at the beach. These beautiful women hoped to catch a rich social worker for an evening or a better life.

If only I had a woman to warm me up.

Povar was more understanding of my situation. After washing in the evening, we drank cups of tea. Very slowly, he started to trust me. He also commanded me less and less. The hints from a few weeks ago helped.

Povar: "I also see that it is not easy for you. But you are still a man. You can lie on the floor and shout that you do not want to continue, but that does not help. Hold on, Baltimor; you can probably leave soon. It is of no interest to anyone to keep you longer."

The guards discussed many topics. If they could not figure it out, they sometimes consulted me as a neutral referee. Professor was most often right when it came to geography, economics, or history. If some of the men disagreed with my input, they said I was partial. They accused me of helping Professor because of our friendship. Sometimes it was the other way around: "You helped Rebel without a name2 because you thought it would help to get along better with him."

Gradually the group and I grew closer. Although our values are far apart, there seemed to be a common denominator that made us bond. Do people bond when they are stuck with each other for a long time? The guards did not have to deal with me. If they ensured that I stayed alive and did not escape, they performed their job.

I could avoid contact with them, but it was to my advantage to engage them socially. My relationship with my guards was a good gauge of my hostage skills.

At the start of my imprisonment, I kept my views to myself if they were against theirs. But the more I did that, the more I denied myself and my culture. My self-esteem suffered, and it put pressure on my identity and freedom of thought. The guards, for example, were not charmed by Jews and homosexuals. In the beginning, I tried to avoid those conversations. On those topics, I tried to avoid straight answers. I measured my words to make sure the rebels could not use them against me later.

Now that I felt more secure when conversing with my captors, I told them that I did have gay or Jewish friends.

One rebel asked, "Do you shake hands with a gay person, is not that dirty?"

Another rebel asked, "Do you wash after sex?" I answered, "Yes, and I guess gay men do so as well."

Povar commented, "A person must try to suppress lust and desires. Since there are gay marriages, it will not take long before the law recognizes pedophilia as normal behavior."

They would never vote for same-sex marriage, and I did not try to convince them either. Just as the Muslim rebels stood up for their view of the world and wanted to share it with me, I stood up for mine and shared it with them. Not to convert them, but so that I stayed true to myself.

I read my three books three times, and they stimulated positive thoughts in my mind. It prevented pessimism and depression. I likened the people in the books to me and my situation. Sometimes I felt sorry for the main characters because of their dire situations. The reading improved my Russian. If I did not understand some words from the context, I asked a guard.

Up to now, I counted 153 days had passed, exactly five months. When it became clear that I could not go home at Christmas, I chose February 2 as the new date. That is the birthday of my younger brother Diederik. I realized that this date was too optimistic; otherwise, there would have been some news. Now I chose my birthday on March 9 as the new date in mind. Fifty-six more days seemed good; eight weeks sounded better, and less than two months seemed best. Two months ago, it was November 12, halfway through Ramadan. Time passed quickly. I could manage until March. Every day I adjusted the number of days. It was a pity I did not have a real end date. That would be easier. Or would it be more difficult?

I had been locked up in a small room for five months without daylight. Our hideout did not have heating and running water. It was so cold that I could not hold my book in my hands, so I laid it down on the bed. The room started to look like a petting zoo with mice, insects, and snails. All those critters visited me. Even a spotted frog came in for a visit one time.

Professor teased me about the frog. He asked, "Did you kiss it? Maybe a princess will appear."

My princess was Amina. I imagined that she was waiting for me. I visualized that after my release, she would be there for me. Then the good times would start again. We would go on holiday for a long time, towards the sun. Just like the old days, we would walk and dance. Romantic dinners and the movies graced our life. I wanted to go to the opera and concerts and take ballroom dancing lessons. I desired to increase my culinary skills and cook decadent recipes at home.

The guards knew that I had a Dagestani fiancée and asked if I protected her virginity. I reminded them that it was inappropriate to ask about someone's wife, fiancée, mother, or sister.

At moments of doubt about Amina waiting for me, I sometimes asked Professor how a Dagestani girl should behave during a lover's abduction.

Professor: "If she's just a decent girl, she will wait. You said that she's a decent girl, so she's waiting for you to come home. You shouldn't abandon her either."

I realized that it was not that important to know if Amina waits for me. I could not influence the outcome. By focusing on her, I had an incentive to keep going. It was better to imagine that she would wait for me. In this way, she gave me the power to hold on.

General returned on January 12 with two new guards. He introduced me to Islam, who made a friendly and calm impression. During airing, I met Peak. His accent differed from the other guards, acted hostile towards me, and brought up the subject of my so-called Jewish spy background. He emphasized that we were in Chechnya. In his opinion, all aid organizations had a connection to Western secret services.

Peak: "Have you ever seen a hungry Chechen? People still support each other here. Even when we rebels arrived in a village, the citizens give us something to eat, even if they don't have that much themselves."

I hoped the guards did not complain again about my suspicious background. The next day I noticed that there was a third newcomer. He was called Abbas. He was very skinny and slightly taller than me. He coughed all the time, and I hoped he did not have TB. Islam had a solid build at about 5 feet 11 inches tall. Peak had an average height and stood at approximately 5 feet 9 inches.

During airing, Islam called me Baltimor. I explained in a gentle way that I preferred to be called Arjan. Baltimor was only for the guards who were there from the beginning. They understood.

Islam was indeed friendly and immediately gave me enough time to wash, brush my teeth, and go to the toilet. He never wanted to know if I were a Jew or a spy, and I asked him why.

Islam: "I do not care. The point is that I have to guard you."

Peak was a better cook than Islam, and he was also the first to use many herbs.

Peak: "I come from Kabardino-Balkaria; our food is spicier."

I did not know whether he came from this more westerly-situated North Caucasian republic, but he did not speak the native language of the other guards. Peak only participated in conversations spoken in Russian.

Abbas only stayed a few days. In those few days, he had told me a lot about Islam. All the guards had a firm conviction of the correctness of Islam.

The guards taught:

- Allah considers children up to fifteen as Muslims.
- Children under 15 can not understand religion.
- A person should always look for true faith.
- A comparison of religion leads to the conclusion that Islam was the only true religion.
- A true believer behaves the way Allah and Muhammad have prescribed it.

- A person born as a Muslim but does not abide by the regulations is not a true Muslim.
- Mortal minds can not understand the mysteries of God.
- Allah rewards Muslims for gaining converts.

General promised to stay a week or two to train the new guards. He wanted to teach them how to behave towards me. He invited me to cook again, which I accepted. During one of his cooking sessions, I taught him how to make an omelet. The good thing was that he added it to his menu.

On Monday, January 19, General came up with the idea to write two letters, one to my parents and one to DWB.

General: "Think about what you want to tell, then we will write it down before Friday. I must go again on Friday. It is just an idea of mine. Maybe it will help you get out earlier and help us to get rid of you. To have you here is good. To be without you is even better."

I was delighted. I could let everyone know that I was doing relatively well. The family needed to know. It was challenging to plan a letter in my head. It was not just a letter. It might be my farewell letter. I wanted to write as much as possible on a few sheets of paper.

On Friday, General finally gave me a pen and paper. Under the watchful eye of Peak, I wrote the two letters in English. At the end of the afternoon,

General came to look, and we started to translate into Russian. We ran out of time. He had to leave immediately after eating. First, he wanted to abandon the plan, but then said that it was also useful in English. There were people on the outside who spoke and read English.

General: "Arjan, don't write secret messages in the letters. It will only hurt you, and you will have to sit here longer. I will take away your privileges. By the way, you will also make me look like a fool."

I opened the first letter with Dear Parents, Brothers, and Sister. I explained to them that I had the opportunity to write a letter to show that I was still alive. In short, I described my fair treatment without violence and that I was fed regular food and had reasonable hygienic conditions. Conditions were like a holiday in our trailer.

Our trailer stood in the middle of a small forest. It looked a bit like a gypsy caravan but bigger. Someone converted an old horse tram into a trailer. The trailer had a small kitchen, a living room, and two bedrooms. We vacationed in the trailer on the weekends or during the summer holidays. As children, we always had a fantastic time. We could swim, fish, play Indian, hunt with bow and arrow, and built huts as much as we wanted.

The resemblance between the caravan and my situation was out of perspective. But like the trailer, everything was made of wood. The toilet was outside, and we had to shower with a bucket because

Maybe these letters will give
the negotiation process an extra push.

What else to write. I think
the most important things have
been said. I am doing more or
less fine although it is not easy.
I have to be patient and
subordinate.
I miss you all, love you all
and hope you are doing fine.
Hope to see you soon.
Please don't blame any one else
then me for the situation I am in.
Not NSE, not America, not yourself.
I hope you also don't blame me
because I really liked my work
and to be in these kind of country
were life is more dangerous than in
Holland

One of the pages from my only letter to my family

102

there was no running hot water. Just like in Dagestan, we had to heat the water with gas from a gas bottle.

In the letter, I further explained that it was difficult to live in uncertainty. Everything would be alright as soon as DWB paid the ransom. I indicated that I sometimes doubted I would come home. This letter had a dual purpose and could be a farewell letter. At that moment, my eyes filled with tears.

My family enjoyed a good relationship with each other. But I had never told my parents that I loved them. Nor had I expressed my gratitude for everything that I had achieved thanks to them. In the letter, I told them for the first time in my life that I loved them. I expressed gratitude for their upbringing, education, and the holidays.

I told them there was more to write, but the remaining space was for my will. I suggested that they share my accident insurance from DWB between them and Amina.

Furthermore, I wished my brother a happy birthday. I told them that I would be patient and that I hoped they were doing well. I indicated that it was 44 days until my birthday. Perhaps this letter could be an extra incentive to celebrate my birthday at home.

I assured them that my situation was not their fault but a culmination of my choices. I signed the letter and wrote the date through my signature.

My letter to DWB was formal. I ended it with the words: "Please get me out of here!"

General left in the evening with the letters in English, and I did not know when he would return.

Chapter 9

Photoshoot

On Sunday, January 26, I was in bed when I heard the radio ring. A little later, Tajik came to take me out of my room. He told me General was coming to take pictures. I had to look good, and I had to shave. Since October, I had not trimmed my beard. The men told me I had a beard like Chattab. Chattab was one of the famous rebel leaders in Chechnya. Something was about to happen. The razor blade became dull very quickly, and I cut myself a few times. Povar and Tajik were sitting in the kitchen next to the bathroom. I shaved with the door open, and we chatted happily, waiting for the arrival of General.

When General arrived, I had to wear a camouflage suit. Freshly shaved, I sat in front of a wall between two Kalashnikovs. Vain as I was, I adjusted my hair. Since shaving my head in August, I had not combed my hair.

I looked like a rebel in my camouflage suit with the weapons and backpacks in the background.

January 2003. After five months the first proof of life.

I hoped that DWB did not think I organized the kidnapping myself.

After taking some snapshots, General and Rebel Without a Name2 left. I dispelled the negative thoughts from my head. Maybe I would celebrate my birthday at home!

As usual, I started counting down. Only 42 days, seven full weeks. Seven weeks ago, it was December 15. From December 15 to now, I had survived, so why not the coming one and a half months.

After taking the photos, everyone was happy and relieved. Finally, there might be progress. Professor had replaced General and was now the leader. He and Tajik thought my release would happen by the end of February.

My brother's birthday passed by without anything happening. It was the third birthday that I missed, and Family days were extra challenging. I had a hard time because, in a real sense, rebels held my family hostage too. My mother and I have birthdays in early March. I probably had to celebrate those birthdays here. What about my father's birthday in May?

My relationship with Professor was getting better. The role of a temporary leader fits him well. The group continued to behave appropriately.

Professor was a bit taller than most rebels with a lean frame and no superfluous fat. He had large brown eyes, dark brown hair, and dark eyebrows.

His mask had large holes for his eyes and mouth, but I still had no idea how Professor looked in his face. I imagined he had a friendly, calm, and compelling face. Professor actively worked to improve my situation. He had the plastic ventilation pipe in the corner of my room shortened to the same level as the ceiling. It did get a bit colder. But due to the better circulation, the smell disappeared.

Professor did not want me to ask personal questions about him because answers to inquiries would compromise his identity. He did not pretend to be Chechen. Professor sometimes talked about the war but never shared any details. Did he have any war details? Although once he had some interesting remarks.

Professor: "You think the sanitary conditions are bad here. I can tell you that this is really like a hotel for rebels. Normally we are always hunted. There is no time to shower at all. Here we can at least rest and recuperate."

Professor hated the Russians because Stalin expelled the Chechens from Chechnya during the Second World War. Stalin thought that the Chechens might start to collaborate with the Germans. To prevent collaboration with Germany, Stalin had Chechens transported by train like cattle to Kazakhstan. Thousands died during the long, harsh journey. Later, Khrushchev recalled Stalin's decree, and the Chechens could return.

In the kitchen, during his kitchen duty, we had long conversations. I did not have to assist him with the cooking, but we drank tea together.

He had a good knowledge of Islam and worldwide geopolitical affairs. He kept me informed about the latest news in the first weeks of February. The United States threatened to attack Iraq. Germany, France, and Canada did not support military action by the United States.

The prejudices against the West were also with him, but he remained open to hearing my side of the story. He would rather see Saddam Hussein leave but without the help of the Americans. Many innocent Muslims would suffer from the American invasion, he thought.

Professor: "Why does America want to impose its culture on the whole world?"

He realized that fanatic Muslims do the same, but that was God's will, and so it was good.

Religion was topic number one in our conversations. Most of the time, I found it interesting to listen to Professor. He communicated well why Islam was essential to him. He had a lot of knowledge about religion and discussed it in an adult manner. With some of the rebels, I felt that their words were just an echo of what they just learned about Islam. In my eyes, it made them innocent and sad. Or maybe they were just a group of actors?

On an evening with many shooting stars, Rebelname2, Povar, and I were outside. Povar was in deep thought, and I was looking at the stars.

Me: "You can make a wish if you see a star fall."

Povar: "They are not falling stars or meteorites; they are angels who shot at Satan with their arrows."

I could hardly stop my urge to laugh. I knew it was part of Muslim religious belief. To Muslims, it made sense to believe all the dogma. Faithful Muslims attributed celestial phenomena to God, a God whose thoughts and motives followers cannot fathom. The faith demonstrated by Islam's followers allowed the spreading of radical ideas worldwide, often by force. The revolutionary Muslim fighters have extra power within them. They are willing to go so far for their faith that it is difficult to stop them. Is it something like football hooligans who, after they get older, usually abandon violence, or is this unstoppable, even as they age?

Sometimes I wondered how an actual fundamentalist Muslim state would look. A country where everyone who lived there was a converted Muslim. A state where everyone wanted to adhere to the religious laws 1,300 years old. Would they create a country that treated the outside world in a friendly way? If it became a paradise on earth, people would join themselves to the Muslim state.

My Russian continued to improve, and I had a better understanding of Islam. However, my abduction was a nightmare and a colossal waste of time. It was also a unique experience. If my abduction did not result in my untimely death, I had an excellent story to tell my grandchildren.

General and Tank returned in mid-February without a response to the photos. General brainstormed another solution.

General: "It is always possible to hand you over to President Maschadov, the Chechen president. He can then release you and make some good publicity. He has denounced the kidnapping and instructed his men to leave aid workers alone. Please cooperate and put in a good word for us and our cause."

Me: "A good word is a bit too much to ask, but I'll tell how things went here. My story depends on how you treat me."

Later we talked about militant leaders. General watched a British documentary about Bin Laden.

I told him that I once read an article about Bin Laden in which his enemies analyzed his photos holding a Kalashnikov. The author stated that Bin Laden had not fired a gun recently and had not taken part in other war acts. They figured this out by examining the well-groomed-looking hands of Bin Laden.

General: "What are you looking at?" General asked when my gaze focused on his small white, smooth hands.

Me: "You don't have real workers' hands."

General: "The author is not right. The callus on the finger with which you are shooting will tell. Also, the bruised skin on your shoulder."

General was very enthusiastic about Bin Laden and praised his support for the jihad. Help, not only with words but also with deeds and financial support.

I continued the discussion at my peril.

Me: "The world would be a lot better with protection against your brother Bin Laden."

General: "How can you say that about our great example."

Me: "I can say what I think of it."

General: "You are talking about my brother."

Me: "It will not be such a nice country if you guys will be in charge. No more free speech."

General: "For the moment, you are in our hands."

I just left it at that. General was angry.

A little later, after we were back in the house, I asked Islam what was wrong with expressing an opinion.

Islam replied, "You may have a different opinion, but of course, Bin Laden is a big hero for Muslims."

I have heard from the other guards that Tank spent some time sick during his absence. At the end of December, he got wounded during a firefight. I could not see through the mask and could not discern whether he looked terrible or good. He was in a bad mood and said he felt weaker.

The next day I felt sick for the first time. I probably had food poisoning. Diarrhea without a toilet in proximity was no fun. Knocking on the door and waiting for a guard to open the door was the worst! Sometimes after entering, I had to go straight outside again. The guards alternated. It was no fun for them to bring me out again and again in the cold. Fortunately, they understood the situation, and no one kept me waiting when I knocked on the door. I felt bad. I preferred not to eat, so I would not have to go to the toilet.

Peak scored a point, "You see that Allah protects us better. We all eat the same, and you are the only one who is sick."

I heard the guards cough a lot. I did not know if they had diarrhea. When it was bitter cold, the men did not go outside to guard.

I told Peak, "You are also *'stampovki boyeviki,'* fake rebels. If it is too cold, you will not even take positions outside."

Peak found the right answer, "Fighters from our other base keep an eye on things." I did not believe him.

After having been to the toilet about 17 times in two days, my situation improved. I felt hungry again and wanted an airing.

It was during the airing that I caught General in a lie. General damaged my trust in him. He first told me something about his family situation, and a bit later, he changed his words. I did not tell him anything about it, but he felt that I read him. I never had 100% trust in him, but I never caught him in a lie until now. I thought we had an agreement about not lying. Why did I think I could trust him? Was I too naive?

We did not talk much in the coming days, and our relationship had cooled. General spoke about the lie during a wash.

General: "I realize you caught me lying. I wanted to cheer you up with some family news, but then I didn't want to overexpose myself."

Me: "You did not tell me that much. You could have asked me not to tell anyone."

General: "Perhaps you pretend to be a good guy, but as soon as you get out, you will betray us. Just like you do not fully trust us, we will never fully trust you."

Me: "Isn't it part of the risk that you can get caught?"

General: "Yes, but we give you more room than the average kidnappers do. Our relationship here is unique, which entails additional risks for us. Close to your release, we can always agree on what you can and cannot say."

I realized he was right. If I sat in a deep basement all the time, I would find out less.

Now that there had been no news for weeks, I was having a hard time again. The euphoria disappeared at the end of February. Out of misery, I started looking for God's help like before. I did not know how to come to Him. For the first time, I knelt on my knees to beg God to help me. I concentrated on the hope of communicating with heaven. By kneeling, I showed more respect to God, but respect for myself declined fast. I found it hypocritical to seek God in difficult times and not in easy times. Besides, was begging a sign of weakness? Did God want us to feel weak and small?

Professor gave me some peace with his words, "It is not for man but for God to judge whether someone is a good believer."

Whether my sincere prayer or by coincidence, we shot another photo. That evening we took a picture of me sitting on a stool in the living room. This time I had a beard of a few weeks. I wore my camouflage shirt. I got photographed with a newspaper in my hand. Not to give away their location, General covered the wall with a colorful sheet.

February 2003

I was allowed to read the newspaper. It made me think of home. Since I was eight, I have always followed the news and read newspapers. Early in the morning, I shared the new newspaper with my father. He read the newspaper's front section at the coffee table, and I read the newspaper's sports section at the dining room table.

Now I read the Iraq crisis developments and read through the economic highlights. Here some bad news as well. The newspaper's financial report did not list Dutch share prices, but the share prices listed on the Dow Jones were much lower than before my abduction. I could not yet pay my ransom. I did see that the euro had become more valuable than the dollar. The good thing was that DWB had to pay less for me than five months ago. Will the kidnappers also follow the economic news and convert their claim into euros?

I used the newspaper as a mop to thoroughly clean my floor. I could see the grain again on the wooden boards.

The atmosphere in the group had improved after the photo. Maybe the image was the last bit of proof needed to liberate me.

During the airing, I felt good and talked a lot. We talked about the date of my release. I guessed it would be at the end of March, two months after the first photo. Tank envisioned the end of April. General tried to calm us down and said that it might take until August.

General: "Then you can see how beautiful it is here in the spring and early summer. You will have seen all seasons by then."

August was far away, and I could not imagine waiting for another six months. I would rather see spring in the Netherlands.

Chapter 10
Counting Down

Spring in the mountains came late. At night, the temperature in the mountains was still far below zero. The sun shined during the day. The sun's angle was so low that the hideout was shaded most of the time by the mountain peak. I anticipated the sun's rays shining for a few moments on my skin again while going to the toilet.

Because of the lack of light in my dark existence, the shortest day, December 21, became a central point in my calculations about my day of release. From the day of my abduction until December 21 were one hundred and thirty-one days. Maybe on May 2$^{nd.}$ I would be free again.

The only natural light in my room entered through the airpipe and the cracks around the door. Based on the intensity, I estimated the time of day. I liked the short days best. They went by faster. Every new day I was closer to my chosen liberation day and one day closer to my real liberation day. I was so happy with wintertime. Soon it would be summertime again. To be honest, I was not looking forward to the long summer days.

The strange thing was that I deliberately fooled myself. In the winter, the men got up later and went to bed earlier. The house stayed quiet longer in the winter than in the summer. The first prayer was at sunset, which was later now. The intervals between the afternoon prayer were shorter. The shortened time between invocation helped my conviction that the days finished earlier.

I counted down until the birthday of my father. Today 78 days, tomorrow 77. Seventy-eight days are more than eleven weeks; seventy-seven days are eleven weeks, seventy-six days are just ten weeks and six days. I counted the same with months. Two months sounded very far away, but one month and twenty-nine days seemed much more positive. My abduction increased the average duration of a kidnapping in the North Caucasus.

My mother's birthday passed, and I reminded the guards that March 9 was my birthday. I knew they did not celebrate birthdays and did not even congratulate each other. Yet I hoped that they did not let my birthday go unnoticed.

Peak congratulated me immediately in the morning. During airing, Povar congratulated me. I did not see Tank all day. Islam appeared to be stricter than the others.

The uncertainty about a rapid liberation grew. I needed small things to make the days more bearable. Fresh snow in the dark moonless night gave a pleasant feeling of loneliness. My little world was virgin white. It was always quiet in the mountains, but the blanket of snow made it even more peaceful. The snow-covered trees looked beautiful, and there were millions of stars in the sky. Islam felt the same.

Islam: "Looking at the sky gives you a sense of freedom, I guess?"

The stars continued to have an enormous attraction for me. At that moment, I felt liberated from the guards and one with the stars, between which I could travel freely.

Peak liked to talk while airing. He spoke so much that we complained that he did not like to hand over the microphone. He still wanted me to believe that we were in Chechnya and not in Dagestan and that most of the rebels were Chechens.

I thought that Islam was the only real Chechen. Islam exuded calmness and self-assurance and did not brag about accomplishments during the war. He peppered his stories with details that his fellow rebels did not provide in their accounts, reflecting the reliable and faithful warrior's image. He gave information on the city of Gudermes that I recognized from my visits to that region. The other rebels praised him as a master bomb maker. On certain days he was relieved from his domestic duties to build bombs.   Islam had a different mother language than the other rebels.

Peak did not speak their language at all. He said he came from Kabardino-Balkaria, a sub-republic to the west of Chechnya. His goal was to live in the mountains in Chechnya. He glorified the country and its population.   To my remarks that the rest of the former Soviet Union thinks Chechens are rude and have a criminal attitude, he responded with a quote from Chattab, "In Afghanistan, I learned to fight, in Chechnya I learned to steal."

Maybe Peak was the only real Chechen. He said that he was also part of the Chattab army camp. He has a great appreciation for the deceased mujahedin. He was particularly impressed by his uncomplicatedness, courage, and lack of hesitation.

Peak has traveled a lot through Russia and graduated from university, although he did not want to talk on that subject. Peak focused on Islam for many years and had joined the Chechen rebels to establish an Islamic state.

"I cannot trust non-Muslims, so I don't believe their historical explanations." He only trusted Muslim scholars.

In the beginning, I didn't like him, but later I managed to get along with him. "My Jewish origins" fascinated him.

Peak: "Hey, Baltimor, it is Easter. If I would have known earlier, I would have brought you matzes."

Sometimes we discussed the role of humanitarian organizations. Peak thought humanitarian organizations did not have a positive influence. He would rather see them leave.

I told him that DWB was trying to highlight the crimes committed by the Russian army. According to Peak, humanitarian workers were spies. He had the opinion spies had infiltrated the humanitarian organizations. I replied that the aid organizations' nature is to assist and that secret services might use these organizations as a cover. I reminded him that a spy who had penetrated his rebel group poisoned his hero Chattab.

From the valley, we sometimes heard the braying of a donkey. When Peak or I noticed the donkey's hee-hawing, we joked that one of our family members was calling.

The relationship between the rebels and me was growing. General had said that I was an intelligent hostage. He had read a report on what the CIA and Mossad meant by quality hostage situations. Our gathering in the mountains was like the situation described in the information. Also, I praised him as a good hostage-taker. Who knows, we might write a letter of recommendation for each other.

The guards had to follow orders from higher up in the chain of command. They all made it clear that they would not like to be in my shoes. They probably rationalized the abduction by "the ends justified the means."

I measured their degree of good or bad by the way they treated me and each other. Under these circumstances, it took a lot more effort and strength to help a weak person. The other rebels laughed at General and especially Professor when they sat in the kitchen with me. The other insurgents did not view fraternization with hostages as a portrayal of toughness.

Over time I built a relationship with most of the rebels. Their belief prescribed that they humanely dealt with me. The behavior of General also gave a moral example for them to follow.

From the beginning, I had profiled myself as someone who did not feel superior to my guards. Occasionally I asked how they felt about me. I mostly wanted to know about their first impression of me. According to them, I was calm and distracted, but also uninhibited, not afraid. I had rarely felt fearful of them. I felt more frightened of an attack by the Russian military or police.

I estimated how to behave without being completely different than I used to act in freedom. In no way did I want to appear weak or complaining. I knew that weakness did not fit into their culture. A man should be tough, proud, and not a sissy. I told them now and then if I disagreed. Most of the time, they appreciated my honesty. Standing up for myself enforced respect.

I only asked for essential things such as extra clothing, blankets, books, and food. Also, I requested to go back to my room before my scheduled time. It gave me a feeling of being my boss.

These rebels did not kidnap me, and I did not consider them my enemies. They did not abuse and humiliate me. In their way, they made the best of a bad situation.

I had the most difficulties with Armen. He acted impatient, suspicious, and stubborn. Also, he harmed me with his lies. I thought his lousy behavior came from a kind of fear.

The other guards had noticed that I had a strained relationship with Armen. General had indicated that Armen was a good soldier. Good warrior or not, I just did not like him.

Kavkazki Krest: "He is afraid of you, Baltimor. When I first experienced you, I saw that you are a good man. He does not see that and is afraid."

At times I was afraid that I would never get out of this situation. The fear sometimes turned into panic. What if destiny put me here for years? The dread left me in total despair, and I walked back and forth with a sense of desperation. I stared at the wall for a long time. I felt the pine trunks closing in on me until they crushed me. Then I felt myself lying in a grave alive. Finally, the insects gnawed at my flesh and slowly started eating me.

It took some effort not to smash the room and bang my head hard against the trunks. I kicked against the wall extremely hard and pretended I was Bruce Lee. The panic attacks never lasted. I could get myself back under control quickly—the idea of committing suicide or provoking murder sometimes popped into mind. But I did not see it as a realistic option.

I wanted my old life back. I did not want to disappoint my family and organization and did not want to let them down. In the eyes of the guards, suicide was a sign of weakness. I did not want them to think I was weak. The situation felt hopeless but not impossible. It was only seven months.

At the end of March, I was facing another challenging period. After the second picture, there was hope for a quick release, but the momentum evaporated. The only thing left was reading and getting lost in my thoughts.

Tank, Peak, and Islam did not make confinement difficult; they stayed calm and stable as a group. Their demeanor gave me peace and trust. It made the toilet procedure easier and gave me more time to wash. Tank had indeed changed since his return in February. He was calmer, quieter, and dreamier than before his battle wounds. He was on the Russian investigation list and had to keep a low profile. He had trouble acclimatizing to life inside the little house.

The monotony of life as a hostage subdued my mood. Every day was a copy of the day before. I calculated how many times I would read the books until my father's birthday. Now that my library was more extensive, I read about seventy pages every day. After reading the first three books five times, I received two new books. With 60 days until the end of May, I could read about 4200 pages. The five books together had approximately 2250 pages. So, I could read them all two more times. Reading the books counteracted my boredom. I pretended I was reading a new book. I made it a game to guess the words at the end of the sentence. I concentrated more on Russian grammar. My Russian had progressed so much that I discovered errors in the text.

It made no sense to escape when the men were around. I would only get a small lead, and that was not enough to take that much risk. I had to flee on Sunday or Wednesday evening. The guards got up early on Monday and Thursday mornings to eat something. They fasted during the day and then went back to bed until ten again. If I escaped at night, I had ten hours to getaway. I did not know where to go but climb the mountain wall. Helicopters flew over the mountain, so maybe they could pick me up. There must be a creek somewhere to walk through, like in the films, to confuse my pursuers. I could walk towards the village and ask for refuge in the mosque or police office.

I also spent a lot of time fantasizing about a plan to renovate my rental house. The plan to buy and refurbish the apartment in which I lived dates from some years ago. It had to do with having a home base. Working at DWB had something of a gypsy existence. The missions were relatively short and had brought me from one end of the world to the other. The work gave little stability. An apartment would do.

In my mind, I went through the renovation of my apartment. There must be central heating. The woodwork must have a different color. In the upstairs, I wanted a new bathroom. I imagined laying the drainpipes, electrical wiring, and heating pipes under the floor.

The only way to escape this room was to break the door. I pulled a long nail from the door. I scratched away the wood around two other nails that held two joists. If I removed those joists, the door might fall apart.

The work went slowly, and I hid the wood chips under the floor and behind the wood-trimmed tree trunks. I painted the scratched wood with resin and bark. It was exciting, and my nerves accelerated my breathing.

I told the guards that Dutch Law does not punish prisoners for an escape. Russia gave escapees extra punishment. The guards made it clear that they would impose a severe penalty for an escape attempt. They insinuated the death penalty was possible.

Sometimes a day went by without thinking about my family. I imagined how they were doing and, of course, hoped that they were doing well. They did not have it easy, either. I wondered from whom my family received support. In a time of need, a person gets to know his friends. I hoped Amina had contact with my family.

I worried about my health, and the weird feeling in my gut did not go away. I fasted a few days and experimented with the food. Sometimes I only ate bread for a week. Maybe the high amounts of sunflower oil caused my stomach problems. Earlier, a filling fell out of my tooth that allowed a piece of my tooth to break off. It did not hurt yet.

Peak and Tank, out of boredom, shot from their room along my door at the kitchen door. Fortunately, I did not unexpectedly bump into a bullet. First, they shot without a silencer, which made a hell of a noise. Then they shot with the silencer, and I heard the bullet hit the wooden door. They behaved with less disciplined behavior in the absence of General.

Peak was the only one that gave me time in the kitchen. He tried to cheer me up with so-called news about a quick release he had heard through the two-way radio. He also told me that he had ordered a game of checkers to combat boredom. Peak also kept me up to date with world news. The war in Iraq had begun, and it pleased him that the American coalition faced so much opposition. He was not impressed by the American soldiers. According to him, they were cowards and fought without conviction.

Peak: "Muslim fighters are not afraid of dying because they know they will go to paradise. That is why you will always see a smile on the face of a deceased mujahideen.   Nor does their body decompose. It smells nice, like caramel."

Peak kept me informed about the attacks on Israel. He happily told the number killed in the attacks. Palestinian suicide bombers killed many in buses, places of entertainment, or markets.

Peak: "Allah Akbar, they have blown up some of your family again. It's a good thing you're here."

I was unsure if he meant it, but his comments about the attacks and his joy were so absurd that they even got ridiculous. The joyful proclamation of these sad events made him a tragic figure in my eyes.

I wondered if something was wrong with these guys. Their sense of good and evil was, in my opinion, abnormally developed. Their religious indoctrination mutated their sense of good and evil. As a result, it clashed with ideas about good and evil in the outside world.

I sometimes asked myself whether it was morally acceptable to have contact with these men. I had mixed feelings. They deprived me of my freedom, but they also treated me humanely. It may be a survival strategy for them to live their life as Muslim fundamentalists.

Peak was full of pride in his perceived superiority of Islam and Muslims. He wanted four wives with as many children as possible. He would educate his children so that other ideas do not contaminate them. If every Muslim had as many children as possible, the world could be conquered and converted. It sounded fascist or naïve.

Tank became the head of the group since the departure of General at the end of February. General was supposed to come back by the end of March, but he did not return yet. In the beginning, Tank had some difficulties with his responsibilities. He was strict with the men and did not take the initiative. Everything must go precisely according to the fixed patterns. At the beginning of April, Tank went to a meeting down in the valley and returned with fresh ideas.

They had the generator repaired, and occasionally I could watch a movie in the evening. One night I watched a mineral water commercial. The commercial showed a beautiful lady who looked like Amina. I proudly told the men. The rebels were a bit skeptical. "Maybe you think you look like

Brad Pitt." It made me feel good to see a woman who looked a bit like Amina.

In April, the weather improved. The first green buds on the trees appeared. For the first time in six months, I felt the sun on my skin again. My complexion had never been as white as during my time in captivity. It seemed I had translucent skin. I sat on the outdoor toilet for a long time to enjoy the sun's rays.

The game Peak ordered had arrived. It consisted of a checkerboard on one side and backgammon on the other side. Tank and Islam did not like playing. Peak had no one to play with, so he gave me the game. Playing checkers against myself did not work. But playing backgammon by myself worked quite well. From the moment that Peak gave me the box, I played non-stop. The ticking of the dice on my bed sounded pleasant to my ears. The first day I played 21 times against myself like a madman. I decided to play the game 21 times every day after that. I kept the score and realized that in the beginning, black plays better than white. But after more than 3,000 times, the score was equal, as the law of statistics.

Peak was still bored and asked if I wanted to play checkers. I welcomed the change. We played in the kitchen, and afterward, we played two or three games in my room almost every night. He was a better checker player than me, but I blamed it on my stressful situation and that he must be a better strategist as a rebel. Peak was always dressed in black, sure to wear a black mask. In the twilight of my oil lamp, he looked like a black ghost. His eyes and mouth were not visible through the holes in the disguise.

Just like the snow and the ground, Tank was also starting to thaw. He came to me occasionally and read something from my books. The guards preferred to read about their religion. Tank was not such a student of theology. He might be more interested in the stories about bandits, beautiful cars, and nice women.

Tank seemed to have kickboxed in the past, and he demonstrated some of his skills during the airing. His kicking technique looked good. As a "boxing expert," he asked me to teach him how to improve his punching technique.

Tank: "We just hit like Kolchoz farmers. You in the West have a much better technique."

We trained on our technique. I had not boxed for ten years, and the last seven months, I had not moved a lot either. After a couple of weeks, I noticed the progress. My physical condition improved, and I enjoyed it more and more.

I boxed with Tank and played checkers with Peak. I was no longer able to work on my escape plans. They always came in unexpectedly, and if they saw the damaged door or wood chips, they would discover my intentions.

Outside, the first flowers appeared. I never had much interest in flowers and nature. I came from Rotterdam and felt more at home in the city than in the countryside. After the winter, I appreciated the beauty of the emerging snowdrops and crocuses. But my love for flowers did not go much further. Even in Africa, I had never gone on a safari. To see animals, I preferred to visit a zoo. During my stay here, I had developed an appreciation for the beauty of nature. At the end of April, the trees around the house grew leaves again. All kinds of flowers popped up around the toilet. Out of the blue, cows came by to enjoy the fresh grass. The scent of spring excited my nose after a long winter in a moist, moldy cage.

The beginning of spring influenced the conversations with Peak and Tank. Up to now, they had talked about sex only occasionally. The men felt uncomfortable discussing sex. With General and Tank, we discussed foreplay, premature ejaculation, oral and anal sex.

The Quran prohibited anal sex but did not mention oral sex. The conversation did not go so smoothly. It seemed as if General did not have much experience in the field of sex. At around 35 years old, he was not proud of it.

Tank did not quite understand the purpose of foreplay. General wanted to know if it was a good sign when a woman was wet. The freer Dutch morality came in handy, and I felt a bit like a sex educator.

General wanted to stay far from anal sex. But after my explanation, oral sex seemed worth trying.

He also wondered what he could do to avoid getting ready too quickly. I explained to him that it was probably due to too much excitement. And that he could pull himself off or prolong the foreplay and get ready during the foreplay.

Peak and I talked about oral sex. He explained that in the North Caucasus, oral sex was reprehensible. It was not masculine to excite a woman in this way. If the municipality discovered that a man did this, it shattered his reputation.

Receiving oral sex may be nice, but the woman's mouth is then contaminated. He wondered how a mother could still kiss her child. Who wants to use the cutlery, plates, and cups of a woman who does oral sex?

After boxing, Tank also occasionally wanted to know the fine things about sex in the West. Besides more information about oral sex, he asked about the confirmation of eating carrots made a longer penis.

There had been little to eat in the past two weeks. Sometimes we ate dry bread or spaghetti boiled in milk powder. Islam had mastered his cooking, and his plov and soup tasted delicious. All winter, we ate fresh meat and winter vegetables. After these months in captivity, I would like to drink a glass of cola again, lick ice cream, or just eat a pizza. It would also be nice to eat in good company.

Since I had my head shaved the day after my arrival, I never had it cut again. I looked forward to Corine, my regular hairdresser, to cut my hair. Tajik and Islam cut hair well. But I postponed cutting it short and did not want to resign myself to the situation. I would have to sit for a long time. How much strength to continue did I have. Did Samson not get his power out of his hair in the Bible? If I only knew my release date. The uncertainty was unbearable, and I felt alone, abandoned, and small.

In the end, I asked Islam to cut my hair. Islam did his best to make something of it. In such a difficult time, a friendly gesture broke me. I sat on my stool in my room with tears in my eyes while he gently put the scissors in my hair.

I cannot control myself. He joked while moving the razor-sharp knife down my throat, and the silliness pulled me out of my profound misery.

Although I cursed my room and situation, I grew attached to some things. From day one, I wore my bath slippers. The top part of the slippers had tares, and I could no longer use them. I tried to keep the slippers together with tape, but it did not work. The guards gave me other slippers, but I did not want to give up the old ones. We started this adventure together and would finish it together. The same applied to my woolen winter socks. The heels wore out, and my big toes stick out through the holes.

In May, the weather turned hot. I no longer needed my winter clothes. I did not wash them for six months, and it was impossible to clean them. I decided to throw away my jacket, sweater, slippers, and socks. I assumed my captivity would end before next winter.

Due to the blossoms, it smelled terrific outside. It was beautiful to see the various trees bloom. With warm weather came flies to gorge themselves in our excrement. They flew into the kitchen and my room. As an employee of Doctors without Borders, I explained the dangers of an open toilet. I could not convince the guards of the need for a toilet lid.

The birds sang a lot early in the morning. Tank invited me to sit outside in the sun in the afternoon while he cleaned his AK47. In the background, I heard chickens, cows, and the braying of Peak's family members.

Tank: "Arjan, when will that nightmare be over for you? Do not count on a quick release. I went down again last night, and there is still no news. General tried to pass by last week, but he got busy with other things."

Tank: "Peak, and I must go on a dangerous mission soon, so I have to gather my equipment and clean my weapons one more time. I'll leave before you."

The news hit like an earthquake. There still was no progress in the negotiation process. A change among the guards was imminent. Since August, Tank had been guarding the house. Although he was not always the easiest, I had come to know him from his better side after his return. It was also a shame that Peak was leaving soon. Although our world views were miles apart, I expected that it would be more boring without him.

Like me, Tank loved to travel, and he hoped to visit Western Europe. It would be difficult because he was on the international tracking list, and his life as a rebel can end at any time.

Tank: "Arjan, I don't have an ordinary life at home. I would prefer to leave everything behind and start again abroad. You can start again later, but for me, that is much harder."

Me: "Amnesty is on the way. Russia had announced an amnesty for rebels giving up the fight."

Tank: "I don't trust that. You know, when I go abroad, there are too many temptations, and I'm afraid I'm not a good Muslim anymore."

I told him that in my eyes, enjoying a few daily temptations did not make him a terrible person, and I did understand that it was not that easy for him. You do not merely abandon your beliefs and thoughts. Giving up your faith was a mortal sin for Muslims.

Halfway through May, while in bed, I heard Peak in front of my door saying goodbye to Islam and Tank. He got a pat on the back, and they wished him well. I hoped he would say goodbye to me as well.

Peak: "Arjan, everything will be fine. You can go home soon."

I was glad he said goodbye. Some confirmation that he liked me was something I needed.

In the morning, I was led outside by Abbas, the tall rebel who was always coughing. Abbas let me stand in the sun.

Abbas: "DWB does not want to pay. First, they agreed to pay five million for you, but now they have withdrawn the offer."

A thunderbolt in a clear sky! A shock of disappointment, fear, and anger passed through me. Anyone knew not to withdraw your offer after a commitment. A few years ago, authorities found the heads of four English and New Zealand telecom employees on the side of the road. Their bosses played games with the ransom. Doctors without Borders must also know this. Even in the everyday business world, you do not renege on an agreement.

Abbas: "You have been messing around with that letter. You seem to have written that your girlfriend knows more about the abduction."

That news did not improve my mood. I was perplexed at the story because I did not put any secret messages in that letter. As agreed, I did not insert a coded message.

139

Abbas: "The negotiator spoke in Baku with your father and a DWB person and said they had deciphered a secret message in your letter. The security services will follow Amina's trail again and have advised DWB not to pay. It is your fault that you have to sit here longer."

Me: "It is nonsense that I wrote down secret messages in my letter. As if I am going to risk sitting here in captivity even longer. Besides, I trust Amina one-hundred percent."

He did not believe me. That did not worry me that much. It was much worse if DWB played games or my father and DWB thought that Amina had something to do with it.

Povar also arrived that night.

Povar: "Baltimor, how are you? Are you still here? It is also your fault, you sly Jew."

He looked at me with curiosity and disgust.

Povar: "Come on, take a bath, and wash your clothes. You don't look good."

I preferred to go to my room, but Povar decided differently. He had not seen me for over two months, and according to him, I had not improved. He took me to the kitchen and gave me ample time to bathe and wash my clothes. We talked a bit, and he also heard the news about the letter and DWB who did not want to pay.

Povar: "You see, nobody needs you. If you were married, your wife and children would have stood up for you. Just kidding, we will find someone else who wants to pay."

He did not seem to worry too much about the letter.

When he saw my urine bottle, he gave me a new bottle. The old transparent bottle had turned completely yellow.

Povar: "So now you look human again."

Back in my room, I could hardly control my anger about DWB. Did not they understand how it worked to get someone free, or did they not want to get me free at all? Maybe DWB washed their hands of me. Perhaps everyone did all they could to have me set free.

Was this the way DWB dealt with its employees? I worked for them for four years, and now they let me down. My colleagues in the field would advocate for my release, I hoped. They could be in a similar situation anytime as well, and would not receive help either. It was not only about me. Not securing my freedom would sully the image of the organization.

Upon my return to freedom, I would teach my director a lesson. Maybe he would understand better if I kidnapped him and locked him up for ten months.

I also blamed myself for leaving the Dutch department. They knew me and the region much better. They also had many more contacts in the area.

General should not have taken those letters before translating them. Then these misunderstandings would not have occurred. Why was DWB not refuting the spy story? Who had an interest in spreading these rumors?

A couple of days later, Abbas left. Islam and Povar did not treat me differently after the rumors. Tank's attitude did change. When I saw him in the kitchen, I asked what bothered him?

Tank: "None of your business. Just like you do not know what is going on. Because of you, we all have to sit here longer."

Suspicion took over again. Even though Tank would soon leave, I did not like it when he distanced himself from me. Would it ever be possible for people to trust each other entirely in a hostage situation?

Despite the rumors, the guards bought new books. I attempted to read my bad mood away. My misery was nothing compared to all Masha's suffering, the main character in one of the new books. Her stepfather rapes her; her mother dies of a heart attack when she sees her husband raping her daughter; she is lured into a porn business by a lover boy, and years later, she endured the murder of her husband and the kidnapping of her son.

However, her misery doesn't keep my sorrow in the background for long.

The countdown to my father's birthday was almost over. The next birthday in the family would be my sister's in August. Then I would be a hostage for one year.

My disbelief about MSF ignorance increased day by day. It may only be rumors, but I was still sitting here.

My plans to renovate my house morphed into a plan to kidnap my director and lock him up for nine months.

The rumors about DWB and the letter took their toll. I would never regain my freedom. I did not have the energy to live my daily routine. I wanted to decide for myself when I went to the shower or the toilet. I did not want to ask for water or food but go to my cupboards. I wanted to wear other clothes. I wanted to see a face again instead of masks. I wanted to sit on a nice chair with the remote control in my hand and simply watch TV. I wanted to eat at the table with friends or family. I wanted to feel the warmth of the sun and the warmth of a female body. I wanted to bathe in the sunlight on a terrace or by the sea. I wanted to feel healthy.

Unfortunately, I could not desire anything now. In Russia, they say that hope died last. Everything in me had already expired, and hope was starting to rot.

I wished General would give me the latest update. At the end of May, I heard Tank leaving at night. I also heard Professor and Tajik arrive. That was good news. In general, we got along quite well. June could turn out to be a good month.

Chapter 11
Letters Home

It was Saturday, and Professor accompanied me. Since the end of January, I had not seen him, and it gave me a secure feeling to have him back.

Professor: "Baltimor, haven't you left yet?"

Me: "You and your February, it is already June!"

Professor: "I didn't say in which year."

While enjoying tea and cookies, he took plenty of time to share the latest news. He asked with interest how was I doing? We enjoyed seeing each other again.

After showering, he asked what I had written to Amina in the letter, so I tried to remember. I did not leave coded messages. Suspicious abductors with a rich imagination may think differently.

Me: "In the letter to my parents, I included Amina in my will. My family did not consider my abduction Amina's fault."

Professor: "Anything else?"

Me: "Yes, in the letter to DWB, I asked them to let Amina know that I loved her and hoped she had returned to Tajikistan."

Professor: "Well, I don't see anything unusual to suspect her. Have you forgotten anything?"

Me: "Not really."

We sent the letter, someone identified something suspicious with it, and I remain a prisoner. After chatting, I went back to my room in a decent mood and dove into one of the two books that Professor and Tajik brought. In the evening, Tajik cooked tasty plov, and I read on. The last day of May ended positively.

June started well. I received some good news. General was on the road with a video camera to record a video. Would this be the last sign of life before my release? There was a lot of buzz from the kitchen. It seemed as if the guards were also happy with the planned video recording. After my discharge, then they could go home.

General: "How are you? I have good and bad news for you."

Me: "Oh, what is that? Start with the good." It was dark in the room, and I did not see his eyes.

General: "If everything goes well, you will be free within a month. If it does not go well, you will be gone within a month, but you will be dead. We are going to set an ultimatum in the video that we are going to record. If there is no payment at the end of the month, we will, unfortunately, have to kill you."

He seemed to be serious. A ping-pong game started in my head. Only 30 days to live and not in the most agreeable circumstances. Would DWB pay if they saw the video? I did not want to die. Oh well, dying did not matter. I had suppressed the thought of death. I knew my abduction could end with my death. But now this possibility was coming close. Only thirty days left in this cursed room, and then death would release me from my suffering. The mental ping pong stopped.

General: "Who is Wouter Kok?"

A shock of recognition and hope passed through me. In February 2001, Wouter Kok was a crisis manager during the kidnapping of a colleague in Chechnya. I was part of his team. So, there was a new contact; finally, some positive news.

I waited in my room. The guards started the generator to power the bulb in the middle of the ceiling. I sat on a stool in front of the blanket on the wall. I told the viewer that I had only a month to live if there was no payment. Furthermore, I explained that this ultimatum was not part of an elaborate game. Without payment of the ransom, my life would end at the end of June.

I did not want to give an impression of weakness and did not want my family to worry if they watched the video. I hoped my performance worked. General was satisfied but did not show me the video.

General: "We'll talk more next time. If you behave, then everything will be fine. Don't carry the ultimatum too close to your heart." What did he mean by that?

They took me back to my room. June was not going to be as good as I expected. It would be my last month, one way or another.

If the rebels did not receive the ransom on time, then at least my death means the end of this spiritual torture. With my death on the horizon, my life flashed before me. What good had the work brought me? I had no house, no wife, no children, not even a regular car. I missed many beautiful and nice women because I found it more important to go on a new assignment. I had seen a lot of misery. I looked into the eyes of death several times. The rebels kept me as a hostage for more than ten months, and my captors threatened my extinction in less than four weeks.

I also reviewed the excellent things. One of my impressive experiences with DWB was my time in Makeni, a small village in Sierra Leone. Until 2001 this village was one of the places where the rebels had their base during the civil war. The government was reluctant to invest in medical facilities. Other aid organizations preferred to stay in the declared safe areas.

One day I accompanied the nurse to the hospital to go on a patient visit. When we arrived at a bed of a woman that had a caesarian a couple of days previously, the nurse literally and figuratively smelled the women's distress. After she removed the bandage, a gaping hole appeared whose edges rotted violently. The dark skin and the red flesh had turned yellow and green, and a colossal stench penetrated my nose.

We placed the sick woman in the Toyota Landcruiser. The stench permeated through the air, and even though the driver opened all windows, the smell did not disappear. At the clinic, the medical staff quickly cleaned the wound without anesthesia. Although I don't have a medical background, they asked me to help. With my nose pulled up, I splashed water in and over the wound so that the doctor and nurse could clean it. Occasionally the severe pain caused screams of despair. The nurse tried to reassure the woman that it was not so bad, and all would be well, but I could see the sick woman did not believe the nurse anymore.

After the operation at home in the village, my face started to hurt enormously in the evening. Because of my aversion to the foul smell, I had stood for hours with my face contorted. My facial muscles had become stiff. Fortunately, the woman survived.

Even here in my cave-like room, these kinds of examples indicate what exactly colored my work. I have directly and indirectly made others' lives more bearable with my dedication and perhaps saved them. I have traveled extensively, had enjoyable, varied, and responsible work, and have also been able to do something with my anthropology study. More importantly, I have always enjoyed working and did what I found exciting and fun. When and if I secure my release, I hope to go on another mission, provided that DWB did not blow the negotiations.

When I sat in the kitchen with Professor, I told him that it might be time to start thinking about escape.

Professor: "Baltimor, we are all surprised and impressed that you have been quiet for so long. You better stay like that during the coming period. If you are on your knees with a gun to your head because we must execute you, you should not try to escape. Escaping will certainly cost your life. As you have always done, staying calm leads to your release one day, whenever that day may come. Every day that you sit here is also a day closer to your liberation. Trust now in God; we do that too."

Me: "Sometimes, I am a little jealous of you because of the steadfast faith and the convinced belief in God. I cannot do that. I always have my doubts. I do not believe in writings from thousands of years ago written down for and by other people."

Professor: "Maybe it will come. The prophet wrote God's word, not just anything. If you are free again, you can always look for the true religion."

Me: "I don't think I will ever become a completely convinced believer."

Professor: "God is almighty and created all of us, gave us our reason, and called us to look for true religion. Do you not see what God has done and still does? How long has man been trying to explain that there is no God? What is the origin of the universe? The big bang theory? Who then kindled the fire to trigger that explosion?"

Me: "You cannot attribute everything that science cannot explain to God's will. That seems like an overly simplistic explanation and shifts away from accountability and avoiding development. People invent new things because they are looking for a better future."

Professor: "Nowhere does it say that we, as people, are not allowed to look for new things. God even welcomes that. Islam has also experienced its peak. Someday the Muslims will rule Spain again."

Me: "If it's up to me, then it will never happen."

We often disagreed with each other, but I did learn a lot about Islam. It was nice to know that I could express my opinions.

The first weeks in June passed quickly. I read new books and played backgammon. White now leads with 54% against 46%. Strangely enough, there was still no room for fear. Hope makes life worth living.

After the toilet, Islam and I often had a chat in front of the door in the sun. He knew that I loved the sun and gave me my pleasure. He had been in the house for more than five consecutive months. We jokingly pretended that he was also held hostage, but with more privileges.

During my captivity, I had not looked at my reflection in a mirror. The rebels shared a small mirror they kept in the kitchen to shave outdoors. I saw the small mirror lying next to the door, so I asked Islam if I could look at myself. My reflection did not make me happy. I had a pale face with greasy hair, a large beard, and a thin neck.

Islam: "Are you looking through the mirror to the forbidden side?"

Me: "The Russian Maffia motto is, 'The less you know, the deeper you sleep. If you know too much, you will sleep very deeply, forever.'"

Islam believed me and allowed me to continue to look further at my reflection.

I asked Islam how he ended up in this rebel group. He knew General from the past and contacted him after he decided to fight the Russians. According to him, Russia wanted to replace the Chechen culture.

Me: "Don't you want to go higher up in the resistance?"

Islam: "I don't want to bear all that responsibility. You have responsibility for the rebels that cannot work and their families."

Now that Islam could not financially care for his family, General must take care of it.

Me: "Are you the bomb specialist?"

Islam did not answer my question. His light blue eyes remained friendly.

Me: "I don't understand why you blow up innocent people. You only get the public opinion against you."

Islam: "You see that wrong. Through this way, we hope that the people will turn against the war and that the violence will come to an end."

Me: "Isn't it cowardly to blow up civilians? Better to attack the military barracks."

Islam: "We try to do that, but it's not always that easy. According to the Islam, if more than 50% of the population supports its leaders' policies, the country is seen as an enemy. Putin still has the support of more than 50%. What the Russians do to our innocent citizens in Chechnya, we do to them in Moscow or anywhere in Russia."

Me: "The support from Europe for your struggle will not increase."

Islam: "We don't need Europe."

Islam had an easy-going pleasant personality and did not talk much. Once Islam started to speak, the guards listened; they valued his opinions. He was never abusive towards me. Islam usually responded simply by saying that I should not ask too much. He did not want to lie. At other times he stated it did not concern me. Islam was the only one in the regular group who had not invited me to sit in the kitchen during cooking or after washing. Yet I appreciated him for his moral behavior.

On June 16, General and Armen came to record a second video to reinforce the demand. On June 20, the middleman would be in contact with people who looked after my case.

In my video, I could hardly hide my anger towards DBW. I asked DBW to hurry the payment of the ransom. Time was ticking away towards my execution. I told them that I wanted to go home again and see my family. I told them that the rebels were anxious to receive the ransom.

I refused to beg. Begging was beneath my honor, and it would not sway the rebels. Chechens were proud people. Chechens did not implore to stay alive as Russian soldiers did during the war.

General left quickly. He must deliver the video on time to the person who would deliver it to the intermediary.

Professor's presence supported me. Almost every time he was on duty, I could sit in the sun. I was also allowed to sit in the kitchen. Now that Peak was no longer there, he occasionally came to play checkers in the evenings.

Sitting in the sun was the highlight of the day. The first time I got a headache from the bright light. The sun and the sunny weather reinforced the desire to go home. I looked forward to the Dutch summer as a free person. I always enjoyed my home in the summer.

I told Professor about my travels. He said he had not traveled outside the region. He wanted to know where Islam had spread. Geography had always been one of my good subjects, and I could tell him a lot about the world.

Dutch history did impress him. He understood how significant the influence of the Netherlands had been during the Golden Age. He didn't like art very much, and although he knew the name Van Gogh, he had never seen anything of him.

Muslims were forbidden to draw or adore pictures of animals or people. That was why the guards removed the wrappers from the cans of meat. People might start worshiping these images. Except for Allah, there was no other God.

Almost any conversation ended up talking about religion. Luckily I had extensive knowledge of the Bible.

Professor: "Man thinks he knows what is good for him, but God knows that much better. God created man."

Me: "Then why does the Koran look so much like the Bible?"

Professor: "It is about the same foundations of faith as that of the Jews and Christians. How can it not be the same? The Quran mentions more than 300 Prophets from the Bible. The difference is that we do not see Christ as the son of God but as a prophet. In the Bible, Christ does not call himself a son of God; that is what people invented themselves."

Professor has told me a lot about the life of Muhammad and the beginning of Islam. Muhammad was considered the last prophet. His word was final.

A powerful argument for the Quran's correctness was that it had not changed since its first writing. The Bible had gone through multiple translations.

Professor: "Christianity is a cunning religion."

Me: "No, not cunning, just the word of God, and that is the All-Knowing."

As I learned more about Islam, and Professor realized more about the Bible, we listened to each other with respect and appreciation, and then we refuted each other's arguments.

Me: "If the Quran writes that Jews and Christians are the only other believers to be respected, where does hatred for the Jews and the West come from?"

Professor: "From the beginning of Islam, the Jews have opposed Muhammad and tried to picture him as a mad man. They have always challenged or questioned the last word of God too much. They also moved too far from the true Jewish faith. Also, Jews do not want to live under Islamic authority and pay taxes."

Me: "What about Christians?"

Professor: "They too have gotten too far away from the right faith. Under Islamic authority, they can adhere to their religion if they carry it out correctly. But some Muslims do not adhere to all the precepts of Islam. Do you want to become a Muslim?"

I must disappoint him. The Islamic culture and my way of life differed too much. Still, Professor hoped that I had the intelligence to make the right choice later.

Professor: "It is even better to make up your mind quickly. The month of June will end soon."

One week before the end of the ultimatum, the Russian army closed in. During the day, I had to pack my things and put on my socks and shoes to join the rebels in an unexpected evacuation event. The guards had a lot of radio contact and walked in and out of the house. I was not allowed to go to the toilet, and I did not get anything to eat. When I could not hold it any longer, they took me out quickly. I heard the exchange of gunfire and the sound of bazookas. The men were all outside. They were on alert but not nervous. They told me the weapons fire was not as close as it sounded. Was it the echo against the mountainsides that made the weapons fire sound so close? I sat in silence on the edge of my bed. I waited for the men to come back and shout Allah Akbar as a sign that the danger was over. The guards explained that we most probably were going to another base. In case of a real evacuation, I had to carry my things and to be very quiet. If I misbehaved while fleeing, they would shoot me.

At night, the danger disappeared. The men and I must pack what we did not need. The Russians stayed nearby. I must give up my books and game. I could not imagine how I survived the first months without books and games. Professor compromised. He permitted me to keep three books and the game.

Chapter 12
Just a Few Days

The tension decreased. DWB promised to pay and wanted a one-week delay.

All my anger about DWB disappeared. They must have had a hard time. Another week and then I was free. Would I see my family again? I dreamed twice that no one else was waiting for me at Schiphol airport except for my family. Of course, the most important people were there, but it was still disappointing. I expected some interest from the press.

I wondered which photo of me the media used. Indeed the family must have picked an excellent snapshot.

The family would be complete again after my return. I grew up in a warm and close family. My oldest brother and I were born on the 10th floor of an apartment building in Rotterdam. Then we moved to a terraced house in the same neighborhood. My younger brother and sister were born there. At the time, it was a new neighborhood with lots of greenery and many young families. As a child, I cycled, played soccer, and skated a lot.

In my eyes, my parents were strict but fair. Go to bed on time, eat on time, do homework, finish something that you started, and be respectful to the elderly. We got some slaps on the wrists, but they meant the best for us. In the spring and summer, we often went to the mobile house and on beach holidays in Zeeland.

As a child, we occasionally had to go to church on Sundays, but after we could indicate that we no longer felt like it, we didn't have to come along anymore

I went to primary school with great pleasure. Our class was a large mosaic of children with different ethnic backgrounds. Quite unusual for that time. Learning was easy for me, and I enjoyed it too. In high school, I also had no problems with learning. But later, a lack of interest resulted in low grades. Then I went to university to study cultural anthropology.

I studied in Uganda about the life of Sudanese refugees. I researched how the refugees viewed medical help from DWB. Then I gave recommendations on how to improve medical service. Since then, I have worked and lived abroad. After my studies, I contacted DWB, and my humanitarian career started.

On the one hand, my parents were proud of my career and what I did, but they would rather have seen my work in the Netherlands.

My parents gave me and my two brothers and sister every opportunity to make something of life. We had the freedom to develop in our ways, but we have also learned to take people and the world around us into account.

We still see each other regularly, get along well, and, if necessary, we are always there for each other. I would like to know so much about how they are doing.

Unexpected, General arrived early in the morning. He was relieved and euphoric.

General: "You are famous. The European Parliament is working on your case, and even Putin is talking about you. Your organization is moving up in higher circles."

According to him, it was only a matter of a few days. He wanted me to look good on the day of my release. He wrote down my shoe and collar size. Also, he wanted to know my preferences for the colors of new shoes, pants, and a shirt.

General: "Are the men still behaving? Sorry I haven't been here more often the last few months, but my life also continues. I can't always be here. From now on, you can shower as often as you want."

Airing and sitting outside during the day had been restricted. Islam, Tajik, and Professor were relieved, just like me.

Tajik: "When you go home, we can finally go home as well. You almost made us housekeepers."

They were a bit worried about what I was going to tell the press and the secret service.

General: "Now that we have treated you as well as possible, I hope you are not going to tell that we have behaved like animals."

Me: "I have already told you that I will not advertise for you, but I will not portray you any worse than you were."

General: "And are you going to betray us all to the FSB?"

Me: "What do I know about you that can be so harmful? I don't know your real names and have never seen your faces."

In the first week of July, we enjoyed a relaxed atmosphere. I washed every other day. I accepted the fact that I had to sit indoors. If I were indeed home quickly, I could manage.

The insects and mice came to visit me in my room again. The eggs laid in the tree trunks last year hatched one by one. It started with large, green beetles with long black feelers. I crushed them with my slippers. I used toilet paper to remove their slimy remains from the floor.

The guards suffered from all kinds of insects. Their best catch was a giant black beetle that looked like a miniature rhino. Professor was proud to show it.

The rustling and gnawing of mice kept me awake. They ran on the ceiling and walls. First, I chased them away with a stick but to no avail. The mice disappeared after I crushed one to death with my slipper. Maybe they smelled their dead brother and disappeared.

After the 10th of July, I realized nothing was going to happen.

Me: "Are you negotiating yourself, or is there a third party that does not inform you?"

Professor: "Those who negotiate are also Muslims; they don't lie to us."

Me: "Are they from your group, or are they like those who kidnapped me from another group."

Professor: "You just have to ask General. He knows more about it. I only know what General tells me."

I did not think General was aware of the negotiation process. The day he came back, he told us that we must be patient.

Me: "General, I think they are stalling you."

General: "Why do you think so?"

Me: "You are often almost as happy as I am when there is good news and also disappointed when there is no follow up."

General: "I still have good faith in a good solution. Don't worry now. We don't want to kill you. It is simply hard; there are so many links in the chain."

Me: "Isn't it better to do the negotiations abroad?"

General: "Arjan, we are good at guarding; others are good at negotiating. Just let everyone do what he does best, then it will probably come to an end."

Me: "Is there a real contact?"

General: "Yes, but the Minister of Security in Dagestan is in the way. He claimed that he almost caught us and advised DWB not to pay. Maybe he didn't allow them to pay."

Me: "Can I go outside again?"

General: "Not yet. You are almost released. It won't take long."

I heard that song before. I was disappointed and learned not to count on their news anymore. General still believed in the assurance of my release. As usual, I held on to good news. Was it a survival technique? It did not matter as long as I survived.

On the 18th of July, Professor left. I guess Armen was taking over Professor's place. Bad news for me. The presence of Professor mitigates my disappointment. To live with Armen, my least favorite rebel, only made it harder for me.

In the morning, Armen brought my food.

Armen: "Baltimor, turn around; I'm without a mask."

It annoys me when he calls me Baltimor because I did not consider him a close friend. The other guards no longer commanded me that way.

Islam came to cut my hair in the afternoon. Because of the heat of the afternoon, he asked me to close my eyes and not look at him during my haircut. His confidence and trust surprised me. Armen came to have a look, and he didn't say a thing, but I felt his negative energy.

Me: "Armen, there are also guys who do trust me. That makes things better here."

When I knocked on the door to go to the toilet, Armen accompanied me outside. Just like the old times, he stood close to me.

Me: "You haven't been here for a long time, but nowadays, people wait at the door."

He walked away, and when I was ready, we went to the kitchen. Only here, I realized that I was wrong. It was not Armen, but someone new. Also, a small guy, but much younger.

He was a quick study. He copied the way the others dealt with me, and he tried to guard me in a relaxed manner.

New Guard: "How old do you think I am?"

Me: "Nineteen."

New Guard: "No, I am twenty-three years old. Married with two children. I have never seen them since the war broke out."

He claimed to have won a target shooting event from rebel leader Basayev. He came here to recover from rebel life.

New Guard: "Do you want to take over my cleaning duties?"

I took this opportunity to have something else to do and got to know him better. After cleaning and chatting, he asked if I wanted to teach him English.

Me: "Come by whenever you feel like it."

During the first week, he showed enthusiasm. He was brilliant and quickly picked up the words. He made a booklet with the terms and expressions he wanted to know. His written Russian was full of mistakes, which I pointed out.

New Guard: "I didn't go to school since I was thirteen."

I more or less accepted the boredom. The books were relatively new. I had my backgammon and occasionally played checkers with some of the guards. Because I was no longer allowed to get aired or sit in the sun, I did not have to wait for hours for those moments to happen.

At the end of July, General returned to take a new photo. I still did not believe General and his group were aware of what was happening.

The photo session was a good example. I held a small letter while the rebels took the picture. The note was used for marketing purposes to praise the introduction of the Euro in Denmark. I concluded that from the EURO2002.DK design on the banknote.

The note said, "Thank you for the video; we have received it in good order. We still want proof of life. Call us on the following number."

General: "Arjan, do you know where this letter come from?"

Me: "I have no clue. If it came from my side, DWB would have made that clear to me."

General: "What does EURO2002.DK mean then?"

Me: "That must have something to do with the introduction of the Euro in 2002. That is a website address."

General: "Yes, of course, I do understand that."

Me: "It must be one of the intermediaries who pretends to be in contact just to keep you happy. I don't think this is from my side. It would have been a paper with a Dutch website address. Time to wake up; they consider you a fool."

General: "Why do you think so? Explain again."

Me: "It has been over a month since we recorded that video, and now, they are coming with this little note. There has been no contact; otherwise, there would be something recognizable for me. Just to reassure you, the intermediary acts as if he is in contact with my people."

General: "I will quickly deliver the photo. It must be at the intermediator before the end of the month."

General left and went back to my room, where I ate the cookies he brought for us. Now and then, there were cookies, but they never lasted long. Rebel or not, everyone in the house liked to eat cookies!

Time ticked by slowly. I had more appreciation for organizations such as Amnesty International. I never used to worry about people who got innocently imprisoned, but now I better understand their importance.

I counted the days to the end of July. It had been 353 days since my abduction. General's prediction about a release in August alarmingly came closer.

July 2003. A picture to verify I was still alive after the ultimatum expired

Chapter 13
Don't Touch My Gun

I called the new youngster Kasparov. Soon he was bored to death with his tasks. He came by occasionally. It was nice to have fresh blood in the house.

Kasparov: "How are you? What is your name?"

His English stagnated a bit. He had no discipline to do his homework. I told him that I did not want to keep telling him the same thing if he did not study. He accidentally left his notes in his pocket while washing, and his enthusiasm disappeared.

English lessons were replaced by playing checkers. Checkers gave us an excellent opportunity to get to know each other. He was a smartass and did not take guarding me too seriously. In the kitchen, he often allowed me to cook and tidy up.

Me: "I guess you prefer to be lazy instead of being tired?"

Kasparov: "No, dude, I do that for you, then you have some distraction."

Me: "It would be even better if you take me outside."

Kasparov: "I don't mind, but General does. I have too much faith in people. That is my big mistake."

Me: "I will not abuse it."

When we sat in the kitchen, I saw that he left his machine gun just around the corner in the corridor. It was tempting to escape, but I controlled myself. Still, I wanted to know how he would react to an attempt.

Me: "I'm just going to get my bottle of water."

I walked to my room, got the bottle, and walked back. Too late, Kasparov realized that I could have grabbed his gun.

Kasparov: "Don't touch my gun!"

Me: "Don't be so careless, boy. Your colleagues can't handle that well."

It was nice that he relaxed around me. I could grab and use his weapon quickly, but I believed in a cheerful ending and saw no reason to put a violent end to it. It was not the right time for it now.

Islam had become the boss of the group. He stayed for almost seven months in a row with me in the hideout. Tajik, Povar, Kasparov, and Professor alternated. I had not seen Tank and Peak since their departure in May and June. I had not heard from Kavkazki Krest and Armen since last winter. Islam allowed me to stand outside a bit longer after my daily walk to the toilet.

Me: "Is there news that I have to stay longer?"

Islam: "Why do you think so?"

Me: "Because I can sit outside again."

Islam: "I don't know. I never lied to you, not even now. Sit outside a bit. Don't worry."

Povar was also present more often. The relationship with him was getting better and better. He frequently asked me in the kitchen. I helped him clean up after dinner, and we sometimes played checkers. He did not play very well and lost due to stupid mistakes. He got so angry about his own mistakes that he hit the checkerboard with his fists.

I had lived a celibate life for a year now. I had not heard the sound of a woman for a year, let alone seen or felt one. In the beginning, it was more difficult than now. Masturbation was less a taboo than oral sex. Sometimes the guards asked me if I masturbated already. They made fun of Povar because he took more and longer showers than the others. But he denied doing it. So far, I managed without doing it. Due to the lack of water and possibilities for showering, I refrained from it.

Two days before my sister's birthday, Professor unexpectedly arrived. The fighters were enthusiastic about his arrival. Maybe he had news? I hoped he would come to me to say hello and share the latest news. After all, he had been gone for two weeks, and maybe he had seen General.

Indeed, he visited me. We played some games of checkers. I controlled my eagerness to ask for news. He knew I was dying to hear the latest update.

Professor: "I came here, especially to tell you of your immediate release. There will be a call any moment, and then you can go."

Will I be home for my sister's birthday? That would be her best gift ever. I also counted down to her birthday. Two more days, it is still possible.

Professor: "I heard it leaked a lot. It is better to take the bark from the trunks; otherwise, they all rot. Just start, then you have something to do right away."

Me: "But you just said I'm leaving soon!?"

Professor: "Yes, but we will continue to use this house. And another thing, Povar is no longer allowed to play checkers. He sometimes gets too excited that he loses. He should stay calm."

Professor left again. My hope increased one more time. It had been less than a month since we shot the last photos. Yet I tried not to get too excited because of the previous disappointments. I must try to keep my emotions in balance.

Islam entered my room the evening after Professor's visit; he had never done that before.

Islam: "I come to play checkers, so I can say that I played with you too."

Me: "If you don't play, you don't have to tell that you lost."

Islam: "We will see."

We played two games that both ended in a tie. Islam left proudly. He was the only one who had never lost.

Professor returned on Saturday, and together we scraped the bark off the trunks because it started to rot and smell. It was heavy and dirty work. The tree trunks were moldy under the bark. In the evening, after showering, I was exhausted. I did not work that much for a year. When I blew out the light, I saw the tree trunks light up. It looked like there was some phosphorus under the bark. In the morning, I showed it to Professor.

Professor: "You can see this in the forest too. I was once shocked when I was fleeing the Russians and suddenly saw the trees light up in a dark forest. After a day or two, it goes away again."

Again, I worked my backside off. It was nice to hold an ax and large knives in my hand. I removed the bark from the trunks and cut away the rot. The room smelled much better. In the afternoon, Professor stopped helping, and I continued.

"Allahu Akbar, Allahu Akbar." Outside I heard the men call upon Allah. I also listened to the two-way radios.

Professor: "Stop working; you can leave the bark for what it is. Allah answered our prayers, Allahu Akbar, Allahu Akbar. General has just called; you will be picked up tonight and transferred to another group. Tidy up quickly; then, you can take a shower."

I would like to jump for joy, but the ceiling was too low. Of course, I could not suppress my smile, and I walked happily like a honking elephant to the bathroom.

Professor was sincerely happy. "You see, everything will be alright. Unbelievable, Allahu Akbar." He muttered a little more and then left me alone with two razor blades and a bucket of hot water.

Professor: "Call me when you finish."

For the first time in a long time, I shaved my beard off. The two blades dulled quickly, and I could not remove the hair without damaging my skin. After shaving, I washed. I did not know what to expect from the new group, so I better clean-up here.

Professor: "You don't look that solid without a beard. With a beard, you come across as much tougher."

Me: "May I have a look in the mirror. I am curious."

Outside, Tajik, Professor, and Kasparov were waiting for me. They congratulated me and watched me look at myself in the mirror. It was not too bad. With my short haircut and skinny face, I looked like a trained athlete.

After dinner, I experienced some problems with my bowels from being nervous.

Time went by slowly, and I fell asleep disappointed. I did not hear the radio. Again, it was not going to happen!

In the middle of the night, I woke up to the ring tone of the mobile radio. Professor went outside for better reception. He returned in a few minutes and walked past my door without saying anything.

In the morning, Islam asked: "Did you already expect that it was not going to happen. You don't seem to be extremely disappointed?"

Me: "Yes, it is not the first time, of course. What went wrong? Fooled again?"

Islam: "General called last night to cancel the operation. I'm sure the next option will be soon."

I kept a little faith and tried to recharge myself. It was sunny outside, and Professor told me that Europe was suffering from a heatwave.

Islam: "People are trying to cool down in the fountains, and they even made a beach in the center of Paris."

Me: "You guys took away so many things from me. I like summer so much."

Islam: "We never knew it would take so long."

Me: "That does not matter now."

The monotony continued. I walked back and forth a lot and did pushups and abdominal exercises. If only I had some paper and a pen. Who knows, there may be a good writer or painter in me. To keep my brain busy, I worked on math problems. Before going to sleep, I tried to remember the names of football players alphabetically. I feared that my intelligence would deteriorate because I did not use my brain.

I have used medication several times against my intestinal complaints. It did not help, and Islam recommended Dekaris.

Islam: "Rebels in the mountains always use that when we can't go to the doctor. It helps against almost all intestinal complaints."

Dekaris did not help me, and I asked for more potent medicines, which they gave me. The complaints got worse, and I had to visit Putin several times a day.

I read how Russian prisoners used chifir to fight bowel problems. Chifir was an extraordinarily strong tea. Kasparov brought me a little bit of it. According to him, I had to alternate small sips with salt. Too much chifir could cause heart palpitations and stomach ulcers. My health was better the next day, but the improvement did not last long.

At the end of August, I could not manage to stay positive. I felt like all my energy sucked out of me. I had been here for more than a year, and the lack of comfort, freedom, and warmth was too much for me.

From the first moment I saw Islam, I thought he and I could get along well. We did not become as close as General, Professor, and I did, but we respected and appreciated each other. We had been together for eight months now. Now and then, I got emotional just by thinking Islam would do something nice for me. Contact with Islam increased the risk that I could not control my emotions. Today Islam leads me to the kitchen, and I dove into the laundry room.

Islam: "Take your time; there is enough water. Pretend you are at home."

He was apparently in a good mood. He always gave me plenty of time to wash in peace but now I could take longer. On my stool in the bathroom, I cleaned my clothes and refilled the water jug as necessary. I was about to cry. I pretended that my eyes were wet from the water.

Islam: "These are difficult times for you, Arjan."

Me: "Mhhh." I did not want to say anything; otherwise, he would know of my choked up emotional state.

Back in my room, I wanted to give my tears free rein, but Islam entered the room. He silently sat down. I tried to control my quivering voice. He let me keep my dignity and did not say anything about it. He was not sure what to do with the situation. He came closer to put his arm around my shoulder, but then he held back.

Islam: "It will be okay; it will be okay."

I wondered if he would tell his colleagues about it. In the days after, I heard no mention of it. Maybe I am too worried about how strong I must look.

Chapter 14

The Noble Rebel

In the first week of September, my life continued in the same rhythm. Saturday morning, to my delight, General pounded at the door. This time I did not hear the change of guards. A promising sign, I slept peacefully.

General: "Arjashka, how are you? You still don't want to leave?"

Me: "Are you back again? Couldn't you live without me?"

General: "I hear you are happy to see me."

Me: "I don't care; I am much more interested in what news you have."

General: "*Oh, ty shaytan.* You devil."

He knows that I feel good when he is around, but it is even better with the news.

General: "I'll tell you more later. I do not have time right now. I have other news for you. You will never see your friend Tank again."

Me: "What do you mean?"

General: "As you know, he went on a mission. He never came back from that."

The news shocked me and even made me sad.

General: "Why are you quiet."

Me: "Somehow, it touches me. In recent months we got a better understanding."

General: "Yes, he had his whims, but in the end, he was a good guy."

Me: "At least he got what he wanted. He died as a martyr?"

General: "Yes, that is the good part of the story."

General and I chatted for more than an hour with the door between us, which made me feel good. Since February, we had not talked much. There was never enough time during the video recordings.

General: "You mix up my entire schedule. You will hear news about your situation tonight when I can look you in the eyes."

The DWB manual advised hostages not to look into the eyes of the kidnappers. In the beginning, I followed this advice obediently. But Tank was annoyed by my behavior.

Tank: "Why are you looking around? I'm sitting here."

Looking down showed submissive behavior in their culture, as it does in Dutch culture. In this way, Tank helped me to stand up for myself.

I reflected on Tank's death. I had mixed feelings. I felt sad because he was someone I knew. Still young, sometimes a bit lost in his thoughts and perhaps also lost in the ideology he stood for. Our relationship was a bit difficult, but he was not mean to me, and rigid as he was, he still tried to make something of the hostage situation.

I also recognized some sort of relief. Tank's death meant one person less was endangering the worldview I stood for. Although he was also responsible for taking my freedom away, I did not see him as an enemy. Did I use his death to grieve over my misery?

General allowed me to go outside at night again.

General: "If I had known you were still not aired, I would have told them earlier to do so."

It was fantastic to be outside again. I especially missed the wind, the stars, and the moon. I was curious about the latest news. General did not want to talk about it, and I did not ask about it.

General: "Don't you want to know what's going on?"

Me: "Don't you want to share something?"

It was nice that we still understood each other.

Me: "Well, then tell me why no one secured my release."

General: "You were supposed to move to another group. Everything looked perfect, but when

I saw them, I stopped the process. I knew some of those guys from the past, and I did not trust them."

General's story sounded reasonable.

General: "I've told you before that I want you to survive this. They were not the kind of people that would properly look after you. Not that they would have killed you instantly, but they were more likely to get rid of you in case of unexpected changes or difficulties."

Was he a noble rebel, or did he pretend to be one? If it was true, then I may be grateful to him. If it were not true, I would never find out the real story anyway.

General: "There are other signs that show a quick release. I will stay here until you are released. This week we are probably eating shashlick."

Me: "Do you have the clothes with you?"

General was supposed to buy me new clothes, but I did not see anything yet.

General: "When we get there, I will make sure I will bring them to the car. They will not get any nicer here. I want you released in decent, clean clothing. I am glad to be back. I like this place and will relax a bit to get rid of the stress. I will enjoy reading about Muhammad's life and a book about an Italian judge fighting Sicily's mafia. I will give the last one to you. There is also a film about an Italian judge named Falcone who fought the mafia, but someone killed him later. I respect that kind of person. They stand up for what they believe."

After lunch, General brought me outside. We sat under a pear tree facing each other.

General: "How are you now? Still going strong?"

Me: "It's not getting any better, but it's ok."

General: "Yes, you act well. Everyone is satisfied with you. You make no problems and understand how you should behave. Are you satisfied with the way we treat you? What do you think of me?"

Me: "Although you keep me here in captivity, I still think you have a good nature."

General: "Imagine it this way. You live in my kingdom with my subjects. I can do whatever I want with you, yet I treat you well in this situation. So, I have to be a good person."

In my opinion, he did not say this to brag. Indeed, he could have turned my life into a real hell on earth. My hostage situation was relatively tame.

I learned that I had a lot of influence. I had control over my behavior and influenced the guards around me. If I was aggressive, I provoked aggression. If I sought isolation, the men would leave me alone. Everyone played their role and yet had their freedom in it.

Me: "You also play a bit of a father figure here. I should call you, Daddy. We both laughed. "Don't the boys call you, Daddy?"

General: "Peak has called me that sometimes."

Me: "I think you couldn't get along well with him?"

General: "Why do you think so?"

Me: "Now and then, I hear something."

General: "Yes, he is stubborn and talks way too much. Also, what he told you annoyed me."

Me: "Did he tell too many details?"

General: "No, way too much nonsense. But you already realized that yourself. You are more intelligent than us."

Me: "In the land of the blind, one-eye is king."

General: "What do you know about us?"

Me: "Only what you told me."

General: "You probably know more than we think. Do you truly not speak our language?"

I had to laugh. Just like I did not trust General, he did not have confidence in me either.

Me: "No, not at all. Will we trust each other?"

General: "Most probably never in this situation. Come on, tell me."

Me: "I don't know that much."

General: "Are we in Chechnya or not?"

Me: "General, suppose I would know more, then I am not going to tell you. Maybe you think I know too much, and will you see me as a danger and never let me go."

General: "Come on, I want to know now what you are going to tell the FSB when you are released."

Me: "Shouldn't we go through that the moment before my release?"

General: "I have thought about that, but I had to laugh a bit about it myself. What if we go through all that, and you will betray us anyway? I do not want to make a fool out of myself. Tell me, where are we?"

It was a bit of a difficult situation. Of course, I knew much more than I let on. It was probably not vital information, but it may be of great importance from the rebels' point of view. I must find the right balance.

Me: "You always say that we are in Chechnya. Why should I doubt that?"

General: "Do you remember what you said when you just got out of the car, and I asked where are we?"

Me: "No, I just asked for my shoes."

General: "Yes, I gave them to you. You said you had not been in the car long enough to be in Chechnya."

Me: "Did I say that? I do not remember that. Kind of stupid to say."

General: "What do you think about it now?"

Me: "If I answer honestly, you must answer honestly. I think we are in Dagestan. I hear cars driving at night while there is a curfew in Chechnya. I am not allowed to see Dagestani TV channels and many of the products we eat come from Dagestan. In the beginning, you too often emphasized that we were in Chechnya. Am I right?"

General: "Yes, you could be right. But for your knowledge, they have lifted the curfew. The transmission does not stop at the border. And the war has left few food producers in Chechnya. Do you also think that we are not Chechen rebels? Do you know how many of us are in the group?"

It would be stupid to lie about the number. General also knew how many rebels had been here.

Me: "Twelve. I do not know who is Chechen or not, but definitely, not all of you are."

I once saw a Russian-Avar dictionary in the kitchen. If everyone spoke Chechnyan, they would not have needed the Russian-Avar dictionary. Avar is a Dagestani language. While reading, sometimes I asked Tank for a translation. Sometimes Tank did not know the meaning either. Should I tell General about the book? It had been in the kitchen for more than a week. Maybe General noticed that I had seen that book.

General: "Am I Chechen?"

Me: "I don't know. As far as I know, you speak several Caucasian languages."

General: "I am a real Chechen. Maybe you even doubt that we are Muslim rebels?"

Me: "I think you are Muslims. Maybe one knows more about Islam than the other, but I believe that you are true Muslims. You know, sometimes I think it is all a big game. That you are all just special agents."

General: "That would make us outstanding actors, and it would mean that you and I are colleagues."

Me: "Yes, but sometimes you don't follow the script. For example, with the Chechen background."

General: "I have not instructed my men what they can and cannot say; that is why you have learned too much. Everyone sometimes talks too much. Because we give you so much freedom, it is our fault."

Me: "Are we colleagues?"

General: "No, you say you are not a spy. Whatever you think, we are rebels. This hideout is really for rest and recovery. That is why it is so important for us that nobody finds out. Russian soldiers always hunt us. There are not so many places where we can get a rest."

Me: "Tell me more about life as a rebel."

He decided to tell how rebels can outwit the police and soldiers at roadblocks.

General: "After being on a mission for a while, you have to make sure you shave before you want to return to civilian life. It is better to have a 5 o'clock shadow than a freshly shaved face because most young people in this region often walk around with a shadow of whiskers on their face of one or two days."

General: "An extended stay in the forests and mountains also entails a specific forest smell that is noticed by well-trained agents or soldiers. It is therefore unwise to enter the city from the woods in one go. We keep city clothing in plastic bags."

General: "Physical discomfort is, of course, more difficult to hide. In hospitals, hospital staff must always report to the police. Sometimes paying a hefty bribe helps, but this is becoming increasingly difficult. Fortunately, there are still some underground doctors, but their number is decreasing."

General: "As I explained to you before, police and soldiers check fingers and shoulders for calluses as indicators of shooting and carrying weapons. The belt of a kalashnikov leaves traces."

General and I enjoyed a pleasant afternoon outdoors. Could we be friends in real life?

It was time to wash. This time Professor took me to the kitchen. Only after I filled the jug with water, I realized he was not wearing a balaclava.

Me: "Put on your mask!"

Professor responded quickly to my remark. In my imagination, I gave him a soft, friendly face. His hairy face seemed hard and dangerous, even malicious. Maybe the twilight made it look worse.

Professor: "Have you seen my face?"

Me: "Yes, but so short that I could not recognize you."

Professor: "How was it? Better than expected?"

Me: "It's more masculine than I expected."

In the evening, I aired with General and Professor. While Professor talked on the radio, General asked if I had ever seen one of the boys without a mask?

Me: "Not until today."

General: "Who did you see today?"

Me: "Maybe that person will tell you."

I did not want to betray Professor. It was up to him to tell General.

Me: "What brand of radios do you have?"

I asked out of interest, but I immediately knew that I made a mistake. General saw it as too much curiosity.

General: "Why do you want to know?"

Me: "I've also worked a lot with radios with DWB, and I don't recognize yours."

General: "It is none of your business."

Professor also joined the conversation again. He did not hear the question about the faces, but he listened to the radio question.

After the airing and washing, I got the feeling that Professor's attitude toward mc cooled. Maybe General blamed him for showing his face to me. I hoped that our relationship would be warm like before. It took two days before he behaved like he always did.

I have often tried to explain what kind of work I did, but no one cared. This time Professor sat down, and I explained to him what kind of work DWB was doing. After the explanation of the basic principles, his interest increased. I also clarified that the DWB salaries were much lower than at the United Nations and the Red Cross.

Professor: "You can even compare humanitarian aid workers a bit with Muslim fanatics. You also leave your own house, give up everything, and fight for the good cause even with the risk of losing your life. If you do this kind of work, you must have a conviction that you can make this world a better place."

I looked at him in surprise. It was the first time that I had heard this comparison. I took it as a compliment.

Me: "Yes, but your struggle is different; we don't use weapons."

Professor: "The jihad does not always have to be with weapons. Jihad can also be done through financial support or just by spreading the word. More people need to have access to the right message."

Me: "At DWB, we don't have a political message."

Professor: "Maybe not directly, but indirectly there is a call for change."

He hit exactly the string that I struggled with during my work. Was an organization neutral if it ignored human rights violations?

Professor: "It is the first time that you have told me about your work. You are enthusiastic. Now I understand better what you came to do here."

Me: "I've tried it before, but I never got through your suspicion."

Professor: "Yes, there are still guys who think you're a spy. I do not think so, especially after this conversation. You know, it doesn't matter to us; we just have to guard you."

I was curious about what General thought about my supposed spy background. We often sat outside reading. He gave me a book about the Italian Mafia, and he read a book about shooting instructions. He did not just read it; he rehearsed the exercises from the book.

Me: "I prefer to shoot with a Beretta."

General: "You said you had never shot before. Are you talking your mouth off?"

Me: "A Beretta 22 shoots fantastic."

General: "Do you want to tell me that you are a spy?"

Me: "I'm just kidding you. I read it in one of the books."

General: "No, Arjan, you can't get away from it anymore."

Me: "You get carried away easily. Just come to my room, and I will show you the book."

He carefully read the passage in the book about the Beretta. Still, he did not fully believe in my innocence. We spent the whole week outside in the afternoon. General always thought that I would receive my freedom soon. I did not count on it. He takes a sticker out of the Quran with "I love you" on it.

General: "This is what someone put in my Quran."

Me: "Then, at least there is someone who likes you."

He once told me that he is not very handsome. Of course, I cannot judge that correctly, but I can make some remarks about it. Sometimes I told him the new phrases I had learned and gave him a "compliment." These ranged from "I can't call you pretty" to "there is no beauty in your vicinity."

The only parts of his face that I had seen were his eyes, mouth, and nose. His eyes were angry by nature. He did not want to appear mad. Sometimes General asked me if his eyes looked already a bit more friendly. We sometimes joked about the characteristics of certain ethnicities. Fortunately, there was room for humor and ridicule. Sharing humor certainly helped me in these difficult times.

We talked about friendships. General told me he had comradeship with non-fundamentalists. But he valued friendships with strict believers more.

General: "Religion binds people on a much broader basis. You know what to expect much better, and the mutual trust is also bigger. I fully trust my men, for example."

Me: "Do you trust me too?"

General: "No, I can never fully trust you the way I trust Professor. You know, our group has strong connections, and we stand up for each other until death. We are brothers by faith. Muslim brothers must stand up for each other. We must avenge each other."

Me: "Is that culture or religion?"

General: "No, those are two different concepts. Blood revenge is also part of our culture, but that is about family. There is also a kind of revenge apart from the blood bond between Muslim brothers. Hence all those international fighters who support each other. That bond can be stronger than the blood bond."

Me: "So you completely trust those people who are involved in my release?"

General: "Those of our group, yes, but I cannot oversee what is going on beyond that."

Me: "It looks like we are waiting in vain again. I don't believe in a quick release."

General: "Arjan, it's not all that easy. Listen carefully. I mean the following seriously. I'll make sure you will come out alive. If Russian soldiers attack, then I will take care of you. Maybe I will even give you a gun to fight with us. Anyway, when the Russians see you, I guarantee you that they will shoot you before asking any questions. We are true Muslims and not allowed to kill innocent people. Next to that, I think you are a kind person, and I noticed you believe I am a kind person."

Indeed, I liked General. Although he took away my freedom and I did not fully trust him. There was something that has connected us quite quickly from the start.

General left disappointed after a week. Will he receive permission to take over the whole process? Povar, Kasparov, and Islam stayed behind to guard me. Povar got a jump rope, and the men were competing. During airing, I asked if I could jump to work on my conditioning. I had not done much exercise, and it felt great to be active again. In my room, I did knee bends and walked back and forth more than before.

Unexpectedly General came back. After dinner, he came to my room.

General: "Arjan, I have been instructed to transfer you to another group. It is going to happen fast now. Within a week."

Me: "You promised to stay with me until the end."

I felt like a child who did not want to say goodbye to its mother the first day at school. Fear gripped my throat. I have been with this group for almost 14 months.

General: "We have to leave here. I would rather have stayed with you until the end. I promised to protect you, and now I do not know what is going to happen to you."

Me: "Do you know those others? What kind of people are they?"

I again realized that these guys had treated me well as a hostage.

General: "Maybe it is better there. I have tried to make it as good as possible for you here. Okay, maybe I should have given you a radio. There was not much more I could do. To let you run around is a bit too much."

I agreed with him. My guards prevented me from trying to escape. If they had let me walk around freely, I probably would have tried to escape.

General: "I will pass it on to the other group how we dealt with you here. I will tell them what kind of person you are. If you behave the same as you did here, everything will be okay."

After General left my room, I surrendered to self-pity. The last month I did not cry, but now it gave me some relief. It was Amina's birthday. I wished I were at her place, sitting at the table with her family.

On Sunday, September 28, General returned.

General: "It is definite now. You will leave here at the end of September, and you will not see this hideout again."

Me: "Have you been able to arrange that your guys can guard me there?"

General: "We did not finish our discussion about that, but it looks good. Tell me who you think owned the dictionary. Then I'll also tell you something later."

Me: "I do not want to disrespect the dead, but I think it was from Tank. In the beginning, I saw him reading a lot from that dictionary."

General: "Yes, that could be true. He paid more attention to the dictionary than to the Quran. He is not dead."

Me: "No?"

General: "As you know, he is not one of the smartest. He asked me to tell you that he was dead."

Me: "You are lying more and more."

General: "How about yourself?"

Me: "Peak once told me that Chattab learned to fight in Afghanistan and learned to steal in Chechnya. I learned to lie here. Do you already know what the new house looks like?"

General: "You will find out; it's better than here."

I was excited. I was moving to a better house, and it seemed that my release was closer. At the front door, I talked to Islam. Islam had a never-changing mood. I asked him if he was ever exuberant?

Islam: "You will only see me exuberant when we have received the money for you."

Me: "Now, you can finally go home again after nine months."

Islam: "I am not going home. I have another task to perform."

Me: "I think you have become a rebel so that you have a good excuse not to be with your wife anymore. Is it not easier to apply for a divorce?"

He laughed about it. I hoped Islam would move with me.

Chapter 15
Fear of the Unknown

It was finally going to happen. I packed my things and rolled up my sleeping bag. My belongings consisted of slippers, two pairs of socks, ridiculously cheap eau de toilette, Rexona deodorant, three books, checkers, extra pants, and a towel. I wanted to take the empty bottles, but Tajik told me that I would not need them.

I could not suppress my trembling during packing, and sweat rolled down my chest and back. Would I move, or would my captors kill me somewhere on the way and leave me behind?

The prospect that I may end up in the hands of a new group did not make me feel at ease. I worried about the treacherous trip down the slope. I remembered the slippery paths and how I almost slid into the canyon.

The guards were also nervous. I walked back and forth, repacking my things. I decided to roll everything in my sleeping bag so that I did not lose anything.

Tajik and Professor blindfolded me and guided me outside. I quietly walked down the mountain with them. We had to walk over rocks and boulders. I bumped my feet and knees several times against all kinds of obstacles and felt blood dripping down my legs. We descended very slowly.

It felt good to be outside again, and I inhaled the sultry mountain air. I smelled cows and heard ferocious barking dogs. After the brisk walk, we arrived at the river, the same river where this group gathered me a year ago.

We had to wait. Then I heard a car and saw the lights of a vehicle through my blindfold. I made myself as tall as possible. I wanted to be as impressive as possible. I shook General's hand as confidently as possible and asked how he was doing.

General: "Good, there is finally some progress in the matter. We are going to bring you closer to Makhachkala. Sorry, but I must put you in the trunk. It will take about three hours."

Tajik tied my hands with a hemp rope and put me in the trunk. It smelled of gasoline, and there were some empty bottles. Through the speakers, I heard some teaching about Islam in Russian.

It was extremely uncomfortable. I got nauseous from the smell of gasoline and the bouncing back and forth. I wished for better roads. After a while, I managed to free my hands and removed the blindfold. I saw some light through the rear lamp holders.

I found the lock mechanism of the tailgate. I carefully tried to open it. Tension ran through my blood. Will I finally be able to escape? Suddenly the car stopped, and I heard another car stop. Did they notice that I tried to open the trunk? People exited the vehicles, and they slammed the doors.

Both cars left again. Did the rebels have two cars? I gave up my attempt to escape. I was nauseous and had to pee so extremely bad.

It felt like we had been driving around in circles for hours. In order not to vomit, I laid as quiet as possible with my eyes closed. My bladder was full. I yelled at the guys that I had to urinate!

"Just hold on; we are almost there!" We stopped at the end of a street in a small village. Through my blindfold, I saw lampposts, and I felt an asphalt street under my feet.

Against a small wall, I emptied my bladder. I walked down the stairs with the help of Armen and entered a building. I had to step over wooden boards.

General took off my blindfold. It was one large building. The large basement was still under construction with a floor of gravel, earth, and rubble. The walls had a raw natural unplastered stone construction, and the basement had a high unfinished ceiling. Wood boards laid scattered on the floor. There was a boarded-up window, and I saw a double-barred door. A big 250-watt bulb hung in the middle of the ceiling.

The bed sagged due to the worn-out spring suspension, and I did not see a toilet or water supply, which made me feel sad. How long must I live in misery? I heard General and Povar talking, snoring, and praying in the other room.

In the morning, General introduced me to Umarbek. He was quite athletic but 5 inches smaller than I. I got my light switch and, to my delight, a television and a video. Farewell to boredom was the first thing that went through my mind.

General: "That is what I promised you a long time ago."

I could see from his eyes that General was smiling.

General: "I have the first video of that Brigade series with me. You enjoyed that series so much. I will buy them all for you."

Me: "Thank you. I appreciate that."

General: "I try to do everything in my power to make it easier for you. I also arranged that Armen and Umarbek would stay with you."

Me: "Where is the bathroom?"

Armen: "You will get a bucket. Later I will install a sink that will make washing easier."

We watched Brigade together, the Russian Maffia series. After dinner, he left again. General was busy with other things. He urged me to behave. I tried to connect the antenna; there was no reception deep down in the basement. I watched the video again.

The following afternoon, Armen and Umarbek came with food. Umarbek explained that General did not permit him to install the antenna. He promised to bring more video cassettes. We had a power outage, so I burned my candle. I would ask for more candles soon. I did not want to sit in the dark.

I reorganized my room. I put my bed against the long wall on the left side of the room. Umarbek helped me reinforce the bed with some shelves from the floor. I swept the loose gravel in a pile with my feet and stomped it deeper into the ground. The floor looked much better.

I hung my clothes and towel on four nails in the left corner near the door. They gave me two tables. One I used as a dining table, and I put the TV on the other one. Both tables stood against the wall opposite the door. The corner to the right of the door would be my toilet and bathroom. There were red spots on the wall. Was that blood? I saw some white, pinkish pieces that looked like brains sticking on the wall. Did they kill someone here? Would I be next? My knees became weak, and my heart skipped some beats. No, that couldn't be true. I had to go home alive. I guessed they just slaughtered some kind of animal. It helped. I became a master of chasing away negative thoughts.

I received a bucket full of water to brush my teeth and to wash. My toilet was a kitchen bowl made from enamel, which also served to collect my wastewater. The toilet conditions were worse than in the previous place. It felt like I was crapping in my own nest. Because I could not cover the bowl, it started to smell. Also, I had to brush my teeth and wash above the dirty water. The positive side was that no one watched me during my private moments.

To my surprise, there were two women and a child in the house. They lived on the floor above me. It was pleasant to hear women's voices. I supposed they knew I lived below. I listened to the same mosque as from the hideout in the mountains. I even listened to the same donkey. I guess I was right about driving in circles.

Calls to prayer from the mosque and the rays of light coming through the boarded-up window allowed me to keep track of time.

I walked around for hours, singing songs. I wore the army jacket they gave me. I had never been in the military but imagined participating in a military parade. Besides parading, I did some stretching exercises.

The sea of space was undoubtedly an improvement, but still, the first few days, I was in a state of denial. Everything bored me. The books made me feel sick. I could not manage to pretend that they were new. I played my game of backgammon once and then pushed it aside. For six months, I played it twenty-one times a day, more than 3,000 times. But now I could not play it.

The improvised toilet wore on my nerves. I could not wash my clothes. All in all, I saw the move as a deterioration of my situation. After a week, the loneliness had given way to acceptance. Umarbek brought me new videos. That was the best gift ever! I watched TV all day, and sometimes Umarbek joined me.

I retreated to my little world with 15 videos. It was 50 days until the beginning of December. The guards said my scheduled release would conclude at the beginning of December. If I watched four videos a day, then I would watch each video 13 times. I had read most of the books more than thirteen times.

It turned out that I watched less TV than planned. Some of the cassettes contained video clips. There was a live concert with different artists. It was fantastic to hear and see music again. I sang and danced along with Tom Jones and the Back Street Boys or walked back and forth, listening to the music. The music brought joy to my life. I imagined how I would dance with Amina and my sister.

Mostly while walking, I could completely shut myself off from the outside world. Time went by, but I was not bored. I absorbed time by counting my steps, watching my shadow, or leveling the floor.

Although I did not watch four movies a day, I still had to watch the same film repeatedly. I sat on an old wooden chair 9 feet away from the television. I made a top ten list of the best actresses. I saw small details that I usually would have overlooked. Just like Robinson Crusoe, I started to keep a calendar. A piece of charcoal served as a pencil, the boarded-up window as a blackboard.

Due to the relative freedom that I currently had, I did not miss my previous accommodation. I had more space to move around, there was light, a television, and I could go to the toilet and wash whenever I want. Occasionally I could not suppress my gloomy mood. Especially the lack of proper hygienic circumstances and food supply was working on my mood. How wonderful it would have been to have running water, a nice toilet, and an oversized bathtub!

The food was about the same as in the hideout but with less variety. The so-called meat days were the worst. The meat with transparent fat, white tendons, and bones boiled in water was considered a treat by the men. In the Netherlands, the dogs would not eat it.

Sports was the only way to eliminate my negative energy and destructive emotions—especially shadow boxing and practicing my kicking technique. When

I got tired and sweaty, I stopped. I splashed myself with cold water and was ready to watch TV.

At night mice kept me awake. They ate from my excrements and then continued to walk through the room. They played with plastic and made a lot of noise. Fortunately, I was a skillful mouse catcher, and I managed to trap them one by one. I hung a plastic bag on the wall with some food scraps. I heard them crawl into it, and I walked to the bag and closed it.

Umarbek did not cause any trouble. He used his judgment. He knew how to look beyond prejudice and suspicion. Sometimes when he brought me food, he came with a new video that he wanted to see. He was not as frugal with water as Armen. Without complaining, he brought water when I asked for it. Also, he gave me enough water to wash my clothes.

In the last week of October, there was finally some news. General entered the room. We greeted each other with a handshake and a cheek-to-cheek greeting. He returned to make video recordings and explained what I had to say. Like in June, I had to answer some questions. They hung the same sheet on the wall. To put some extra pressure on the negotiations, I suggested him to hit me in the face a few times. It seemed like a good idea, but we rejected it anyway. I did not feel like having a black eye again, and he did not feel like doing it either.

Me: "Use charcoal to put some shadow around my eyes, so it looks like I have two black eyes."

General liked the idea and turned out to be a good makeup artist, and we started the recording.

The prospect of release by the beginning of December gave me the power and courage to hold on. In a week, Ramadan would start. One month of fasting, and then hopefully, I would go home.

In the other room, I had seen a barbell that no one was using. General didn't mind me using it. With lots of enthusiasm, I started exercising three times a day.

General tightened the house rules. When the men came with food or collected my droppings, I had to stand in the corner. I had to turn my face to the wall and extend my hands against the wall above my head. Umarbek was no longer allowed to watch television with me.

The end of October got closer, and I lived the same pattern every day of sleeping, watching TV, exercising, and eating. The most important thing was that I got more confident that I would survive.

Forty days until the end of November, then I could go home. Numbed by the redundancy of my life, I lived in my world.

Chapter 16
The Television

Ramadan was going well. Fasting, a regular schedule, and going to the toilet by myself had a good effect on my health. The weird feeling in my lower abdomen had almost subsided. Early in the morning, I did my fitness exercises, ate breakfast, and then slept until early afternoon.

I received two videos with religious content during Ramadan. One was about the universe and the other about the life of the prophet Muhammad.

I felt like an airplane on an undisturbed autopilot. I flew high without being troubled by turbulence. The numbness ensured that I felt comfortable. Negotiations about my release seemed to be going well.

Armen: "It looks like you're at home before the end of the year. Although, of course, it always depends on the will of God. Baltimor, I hope you understand that we have nothing against you. No one wants to be in your position. But keep it up for a while."

These were words I had heard before, but for the first time from Armen. He started to act as a compassionate person. As usual, religion was the catalyst for our rising relationship. Participating in Ramadan and my Christian background also helped. His spiritual development had not stood still in recent months either.

The temperature dropped slowly. In the basement, it was quite cold. Luckily, there was electricity in this house, and Armen was bringing a heater. With no television reception, I decided to put the TV closer to the window. Now I could put the heater in the window frame as an antenna. It worked, and I received one of the two Russian state channels. The image was not sharp. I would call the cable tv provider at home, but the reception was good enough to follow the programs. I now had real television instead of videos. I just had to be careful that the guards did not find out. Fortunately, they had to open two doors before they arrived at my barred door.

Cunning as a fox, I let a video play with more or less the same program that I watched. The disadvantage was that I could not use the heater while watching.

Umarbek: "We also want to see the last films you received. You will have to do without television for a while."

Umarbek disturbed the fun and my inner peace.

Me: "Will I get it back?"

Umarbek: "Yes, when we finish watching. It doesn't take that long."

In the evening, he took the television away. I was devastated. Umarbek robbed me of my most precious possession, which made me feel like a kid who got his favorite toy taken away. Like the child, I had tears in my eyes from anger and incomprehension. I sulked on my bed. I could go on a hunger strike or throw the bucket with my droppings in my room. Anyway, I had to deal with my misery. In short, I had to accept my destiny and remain calm.

It took a while to calm down. I opened a book again and tried to read. Not that I had forgotten the story, but I had not read a book for more than a month. The interest in the book's story returned. It was the music that I missed the most. While exercising and running back and forth, I always had the music on in the background.

Every time they brought food, I asked if they were bored yet.

They answered, "No, we are busy? But we will bring it back soon."

After about four days, the television returned. They decided that I could watch during day time and they would watch it at night.

It was so cold that I had to turn on the heater. So, I could not watch Russian television. I received a new stove, and they took away the old one. I lost my antenna, but soon I noticed that the new heater functioned as an antenna. There was perhaps even more progression. With Umarbek's nail clipper, I cut a piece of electrical wire from the stove, and indeed it worked great without the furnace itself. Now I could watch television in a well-heated room. I felt like MacGyver, an old television hero. It was nice to have contact with the outside world and to follow the news.

Ramadan concluded for another year. Once again, it was not difficult to take part; it was even pleasant. Whether it came from fasting, physically, I felt better than a month ago. Mentally I slowly got out of balance again. November was almost over, and there was no news.

Because of sharing the TV, I was again dependent on the three books I had owned since the end of June. I knew them by heart. I had to make all my requests to Armen several times before anything was bought or brought. General had already scolded him one time on my behalf. If I asked for something that I had in the past, he must purchase it for me—such as toilet paper, candles, and lighters.

Me: Maybe you can ask General to bring the other books?

Armen: "You still have books."

Me: "Does it not occur to you that I may have read them already?"

Armen: "Yes, but haven't you read the other ones?"

Me: "Yes, but I have been reading these since June. Just like someone else is reading those books."

Armen: "We don't read that nonsense."

Me: "Just like I would buy books like that in my spare time. Here they come in handy for me."

Armen: "I will ask again."

Me: "If you do not watch the TV, leave it here."

Armen: "We are bored too. You have watched those videos already so many times."

Me: "I like the music video."

Armen: "Music comes from Satan, that is not good for you."

Me: "As you know, I don't believe as you do."

Armen: "If you did that, you would be home sooner."

Me: "God is not helping you either. How long have you been waiting for your money now? At least 13 people have been unable to do anything else for more than a year."

Armen: "How do you know how many people we are?"

He did not realize how stupid he was from time to time. If he thought for a moment, he would know that I had seen at least 13 different men.

My lack of news and the sharing of television made my mood worse. I understood that the guys also wanted to watch TV. It was hard to get used to the boredom again. I read the books reluctantly and continued to exercise.

Out of discontent, I started thinking about escaping. I tried to dig a hole under the wall. With fresh courage, I scoured the stones, debris, and the earth with my hands. Scratching resulted in bleeding fingertips and black dirt under my nails. I hid the rubble under the shelves and in the holes in the wall. Then I remembered the construction methods in Dagestan. First, they dug a hole in the ground. Then they built the walls on the inside of the hole. Finally, they filled the space between the walls with debris, and the foundation was ready. I could never have dug myself out.

Armen and Umarbek unexpectedly removed the television during the day. I just started to watch an excellent movie and did not expect them until early in the evening.

Armen: "A good film will be on TV; you will get it back later."

Me: "Isn't it a bit early."

Armen: "You don't have to look so sour. We will bring it back."

I gave up and walked away from the door, and Armen and Umarbek left the cellar. I was furious. I sat on the bed and complained about everything and everyone. The first door opened again, and Armen stood in front of bars.

Armen: "Baltimor, don't wind up like that now. We do not keep the TV that long. Try to empathize with us now. We are bored too."

Me: "Yes, but you can leave, and it seems that I will never leave."

Armen: "Everything is still going well. The big news is coming soon."

Me: "Can't we stick to the old agreement? I watch until the evening prayer and you afterward. I do not mind sharing. The unexpected taking of the TV gets me out of my rhythm."

I needed consistency to get through this. Armen understood and agreed.

Chapter 17
Second Christmas in Captivity

Armen kept his word. He let me watch television during the day, and he watched it in the evening. Armen handed me all my books, and I started one of the books that I had not read for almost half a year. I had little trouble lifting the heavy dumbbell. I was curious about how my physique looked after training intensely three times a day for one and a half months.

Two more weeks, and then it was my second Christmas in captivity. Russian television counted down to New Year's Day, 23 days to go. This year they will get me out.

I followed the news and a Russian soap opera. Jihadists continued to blow up buses in Israel. Putin's party had won the elections in Russia, and Georgia had a new president after a revolution. I was back in a steady rhythm.

Tuesday, December 9, early in the morning, Armen woke me up.

Armen: "Baltimor, get your things together quickly. We are moving!"

He looked at me through the barred door, and I saw his eyes shine.

Armen: "I told you that your release would happen soon."

Me: "Really?"

Armen: "General will come soon, he will tell all about it. Just hurry up!"

I rolled my things in the mattress. I also took my two bottles. I rolled up the antenna and hid it in a hole in the wall. Maybe we would come back again. Full of expectations, I waited. Was my nightmare finally over? Would I be home before Christmas? I was nervous. Anything could happen en route. Maybe a sniper would shoot me on the way to the airport. Armen knocked again.

Armen: "It is canceled. General just called."

Me: "Was it about moving, or was it because we almost had to flee the Russian Army?"

Armen: "What do you mean?"

Me: "In the mountains, we were sometimes about to move because the Russians were close."

Armen: "No, that's not the case now."

I unpacked my things, put my mattress on my bed, and fell asleep. When I woke up, I was not upset. The positive news evaporated so quickly; I did not have time to get out of balance.

On TV, I saw the release of a young boy in Dagestan after three years of abduction. I imagined captivity for another 18 months. I wondered if I could survive. The young boy hardly did; he looked like a skeleton.

Armen: "Are you looking at those music clips again?"

I did not notice Armen came in. Just in time, I switched the TV to video.

Armen: "Can't you get enough of it? Pack your things; we will give it another try. General will be here soon."

I packed my things. Within a few minutes, General stood at the door without saying anything. He was curious if I would recognize him.

Me: "Hey, General."

He slapped his hands together as if he was disappointed that I recognized him.

General: "It is not a good sign that you still recognize me. Will you ever forget me?"

He tried to come in, but the lock would not open.

General: "Did you break it?"

Me: "Not that I know of. Armen had trouble locking the door this afternoon."

General used a crowbar to break the lock and entered. Tajik was also there, and we all shook hands.

General: "We will move again. From there, they will pick you up, and you can finally go home. It won't take more than a week."

They moved my things, the television, and videos first. I had to wait for the second round. I was nervous and not excited because I had my doubts about this whole operation. Last Tuesday's postponement did not portend anything good.

I was blindfolded and had to walk to the car. It was the first time in more than two months that I was outside. Winter had started; it was cold out. I had to sit in the back seat. Someone was already in the car, but I did not recognize him. Tajik got on the other side, and we drove away. I was even more nervous now, just like the guys next to me. They did not talk, and I heard their breathing. They did not take it out on me as the kidnappers did during the transfer a week after my kidnapping. Instead of getting some blows against my head General gave me a Mars candy bar.

Me: "Is there snow already?"

General: "Yes, the road is very slippery. Do you know what kind of car you are in?"

Me: "It is certainly not a Mercedes 600."

The three of us sat hip to hip in the back seat. The Kalashnikovs that hung over the shoulders of the men took up much-needed space. I would rather not lose anything. I just got winter clothes, and if we moved to a house without electricity, they would come in handy.

After a smooth ride of 30 minutes, we arrived at the new accommodation. I was quickly pulled out of the car and pushed inside. I was curious; will my situation improve? Still blindfolded, I had been leaning against a sink for about ten minutes. I did not dare to move. I felt the heat of a stove, and I did not want to get burned. I wondered who would be here.

Povar: "Please be patient."

Me: "Were you in the car too? I didn't recognize you." I look for his hand; he took it: "You haven't got rid of me yet."

They took my blindfold off, and I saw a steep iron staircase that went down below the room. This room could not be mine!

General: "It is only for a few days. Then you are out of here."

I carefully walked down the stairs into the dark cell. I saw nothing and felt humiliated. In my disappointment and panic, I asked for my things. I wanted the candles and bottles close to me.

I lit the candle. It was a storage space or crawl space of 6.6 feet by 4 feet with a height of just 5 feet. I could not even stand up straight. There were two pillows from a demolished couch. Also, there were bags of sawdust.

It seemed they prepared the storage area for my stay. It was freezing, and I quickly crawled into my army sleeping bag. The sleeping bag was not thick enough to warm me properly. With my one candle, I went to sleep.

I heard cars and trucks drive by, so we had to be on an extensive transit route. The house was probably at a crossroads. Many cars and trucks turned off the main road.

General called me upstairs in the morning to have breakfast.

General: "Hurry up; the food is getting cold. Come up, it is better here, or perhaps you don't feel like sitting with us."

There were four rebels. Kasparov joined them, and Tajik had left. Too bad, Armen was still there.

General: "Don't you want to greet Arjan?"

Kasparov didn't say much.

General: "Are you shy or something. Say hello to him. You got along well."

General tried to break the ice.

There were baked potatoes with onions and fat-cooked meat. I did not want the meat cooked in oil in this miserable situation, so I did not eat much. The less I had to go to the toilet, the better.

General tried to make it more pleasant for me. He brought chips and cookies that looked like old fashioned cell phones.

Kasparov: "You are not allowed to call; remove the antennas, then they won't work anymore."

General promised that I could watch new videos between prayers. The guards organized their new accommodation, and I set-up my crawl space. It felt like a grave. Fortunately, I received a heater, which made me feel better.

A little later, the rebels invited me to come up. While lying between the guards, I watched Gladiator for the twentieth time.

General and I talked a lot. Povar and Kasparov occasionally contributed to the conversation. It seemed like a reunion; the atmosphere was the same as two months ago. I saw the surprise on Armen's face when he noticed how we socialized.

General: "Your girlfriend still cares about you. Isn't her name Amina?"

Me: "Yes, how do you know?"

General: "You said so yourself."

Me: "No, not her name, that she still cares about me?"

General: "It was in the newspaper. She is collecting signatures for you. In Dagestan, 40,000 people have signed for your release. People say it is a shame that someone who comes to do good in their country is held hostage for such a long time."

To hear about Amina for the first time in all these months made me happy. I always imagined that she would wait for me, and now it appeared to be so. Poor girl, she did not know if I would ever come back alive.

Kasparov led me to another room. The room looked like a mess with old rusted tools and a workbench in the middle, probably an abandoned workshop. The guards constructed a provisional toilet out of a bucket and bags filled with sawdust behind the workbench, and they included additional buckets and some water to wash. There was no running water here either. All we had was the water supply in the milk cans.

Professor once explained that the sanitary facilities in the mountain hideout were excellent by rebel standards. I doubted his words and rebel existence, but now I see that it could be the truth.

Back in the so-called living room, General asked what I thought of the house. I told him it looked like a ruin.

General: "Arjan, I have made a deal with people to get you free. I run many risks myself, but it seemed to be the only way to finally bring this bizarre part of our lives to a close. We are near the main road, and the transfer point is nearby. Please hold on."

I still didn't trust it. If we were close to a transfer point, the General would have known precisely the transfer time.

The first three days passed fast. General's presence mitigated the Spartan circumstances. I spent a lot of time with the men in the living room, and when I sat downstairs, I read. Mice currently caused the most nuisance. They probably came to eat the food. They were so hungry that their vigilance dropped. I caught seven mice in no time.

The men had no trouble guarding me at night. My basement had thick concrete walls, and the guards slept on the hatch door. I had no urge to escape. That would show a lack of intelligence in this final phase. General knew that too. That was why he tried to create a relaxed atmosphere.

Occasionally an older man came by to bring water. When he arrived, I had to go into my crawl space. I supposed he did not know about my presence because of the window coverings made of sheets in the living room. The house had probably been vacant for a long time. Probably the locals would have noticed the lights already. Sometimes when cars parked in front of the house, the men switched off the TV.

I was tense. The tension and inadequate toilet facilities hit my gut. The same misery as in the mountains started all over again. General was more miserable too. His failure to expedite my freedom broke his pride. I talked to him while I washed.

General: "Tonight, Armen, and I will leave and find out what is going on."

Me: "When should my release happen?"

General: "It should have happened already. As you can see, we are not safe here either. It is not how I wanted it to happen."

Me: "Have you asked your boss already if you can do the negotiations yourself?"

General: "If your release fails again, I will certainly do that."

Me: "Maybe that's better. We can work out the plan that we devised in the fall."

There was a large mirror in the bathroom, and I wanted to see how I looked naked these days. I had not seen a complete view of myself for 16 months.

Me: "Turn around; I want to look at myself in the mirror."

General turned around, and I looked at myself. The fitness training showed some results. I looked more muscular than before, but I lost a lot of weight. If I lost more weight, I would look like a concentration camp prisoner. Yet it was nice to see progress.

General: "You look a lot sportier than when you came. It has not made you worse."

Me: "What do you mean better? I am a lot thinner."

General: "Yes, when you arrived, you had a passive office body. After two months of fitness training, you look fit. Just look at your arms!"

My arms looked better than before, but my shoulders, legs, and buttocks did not. General's compliments felt good. I remembered, "The love of a woman does not go through the stomach but through the ears."

In the next few days, I had to stay in the crawl space more than before. General had left, and the guards were not that keen to take me out.

General returned on Monday night, Professor and Tajik alternated guard duty with Povar and Kasparov. They greeted me through the hatch.

General: "Tomorrow will be a long day, so rest well."

Me: "Is there any news?"

General: "Yes, but not what you want to hear, unfortunately, no shashlick."

In the morning, I saw Professor; we had not seen each other for two months. We caught up in the laundry room.

Professor: "General will soon make a video of you. He is leaving again tonight."

General indeed wanted to record a video. He was visibly disappointed that the transfer did not take place.

General: "The police and security services are always in the way. The Minister of Internal Affairs said that he thinks he can resolve the matter before the 27th of January. He has again asked DWB not to interfere with the case until that date. Later they can then start through their channels. It seems as if they are listening to the minister again. My bosses are fed up with that behavior and have said that I must decide what to do with you. You are no longer of use to them."

For a moment, I did not know what to say. If I were no longer useful, the rebels could decide to kill me!

Me: "So, why not release me without a ransom? Do a publicity stunt with your president Maschadov to improve his image."

I just said whatever came to mind. My brain worked fast. I stayed calm but wanted to say a lot of things at the same time. General was ahead of me.

General: "That sounds good to you. It means you can go home. But what about us? Maschadov has forbidden us from abducting aid workers. He will punish us."

Me: "In the first place, you did not abduct me. But yes, we can resolve this situation in a positive way for all of us. I don't mind if you earn a bit of money."

The rebels tried to make my incarceration bearable, and if General freed me without a ransom, in their view, my release would have an anticlimactic conclusion. The alternative could jeopardize my life. Let DWB bleed and feel the pain. They had their responsibility as an employer. DWB had enough money and could spread the ransom over fiscal years 2002, 2003, and 2004. It was not only about my life. How about the ideals they defended?

Did I suffer from Stockholm syndrome? Had I befriended my abductors and sympathized with their ideals? No, I certainly did not sympathize with their standards. I got along well with some of the kidnappers. It was about respect and appreciation, but it was not friendship.

General: "I've said it before, I don't want you to be left dead here either. But I cannot guarantee your safety. If there is a raid, you probably face certain death."

Me: "What is your intention? Shoot another video and give it to your friends and wait in vain?"

General: "Yes, I want to try again. I heard that there is someone here in Dagestan who has known your father for a long time. I want to give that video to your father through him."

Me: "I sincerely doubt that my father knows someone here. That someone must have a new relationship with my father because he did not know anyone from Dagestan. Maybe they try to fool you?"

General: "No, this should work; let's try."

Me: "Why my father?"

General: "Your family is the only party involved that wants to have you free. I have my doubts about DWB and FSB."

Me: "What am I supposed to say in that video?"

General: "You have to explain our preparation and organization as rebels. That you really cannot escape because we always walk around with weapons. If there is a raid, you will die first. It is shameful for Chechens to release a hostage without money. You must explain to your father that the FSB would rather not have those 5 million euros in rebels' hands because we will use the money to fight against Russia. They can, therefore, not be trusted. They probably do not want a happy ending. Explain that DWB may prefer not to pay. They now act as if they want to pay, but they do not cross the bridge. They hide behind the Dagestan security services. Who knows, they might work with the FSB. If they want to pay so badly, have them give the money to your father. He can arrange it with his contacts in Dagestan."

Me: "Sounds reasonable. Yet it seems doubtful that my father has good contacts here. He did not have any in the past. How can that guy be trusted?"

General: "We warned him that his family would die if he tries to betray us."

Me: "Maybe I should say that it is better to negotiate abroad. Natives of the Caucasus, notice DWB or any foreigner immediately."

General: "Your father's acquaintance knows how to do it. He travels a lot."

Me: "I think you should do it without that person. Just send one of your groups to Turkey or Azerbaijan and have my family contact you. I do not trust that so-called acquaintance."

General: "It will be okay. Come on. You will not have to sit in this basement for long. We will be moving again soon."

Christmas 2003 was even worse than Christmas in 2002. I spent most of the day in the twilight of the crawl space. It hurt to celebrate Christmas like this. Fortunately, I got some calluses on my soul. It must be horrible for my family to celebrate Christmas again without their son and brother. Will they celebrate it? Are they all sitting together with an empty plate and one empty chair for me?

In the evening, there was better news; we were moving again. The accommodations improved significantly in the new house. I got a neat and spacious bedroom with light and a heater. The furnished living room had a table, a couch, and two armchairs. I could not wait to sit on the furniture. I had not been in a comfortable chair for sixteen months. There was no running water here either, but there is a separate bathroom with a bathtub. The house also had a long corridor and a vacant room where General allowed me to do my exercises.

The toilet, which I was only allowed to visit in the dark, was outside in a shed. I did not want to think about that for a while, although I could imagine it.

There was plenty to eat again. We ate fresh meat, chocolate, carrots, cabbage, potatoes, and lots of bread and cheese. Christmas ended a lot better than it started. Is it a sign from God above, or is it just a coincidence that we had to move to a better house today?

My bed was soft, and I laid my mattress on the floor. I slept well, and in the morning, the men served a good breakfast with bread, fried eggs, meat, and onions.

I had a desk with a luxurious wooden chair with a soft seat. In all this time, I had not been so comfortable.

The days between Christmas and New Year's day were relatively pleasant. I enjoyed bathing so much! For the first time in six weeks, I could finally clean myself thoroughly. My clothes were also clean again.

Professor and Tajik trusted me, and I occasionally cooked whatever I wanted. It was nice to stand alone in the bathroom and kitchen, and I did not have to pay attention to the amount of noise I made. I enjoyed time in the kitchen with Professor and Tajik, chopping vegetables, and meat.

There was a mirror in the bathroom, and I had ample time to look at myself. I needed to train more but did not have a barbell anymore. Instead, I increased the number of abdominal exercises.

Time flew by. I exercised, read a lot, and watched television with the men. There were many Christmas movies. I was sitting comfortably in an overstuffed chair. I was glad that the men accommodated me and sat for hours with their masks on.

Just before the end of the year, Tajik forgot to wear his mask while bringing my food. After I told him it is better to wear a mask, he asked:

Tajik: "Do I look better than Professor?"

Me: "I don't know; I've never seen Professor's face properly."

Tajik: "Is it friendly or frightening?"

Me: "It's kind of friendly. I expected an unkind face because of your voice."

Tajik: "The guards have new videos about the war in Chechnya."

I saw images of Chechen fighters cutting the throats of Russian soldiers. There were also images of Chechen rebels blowing up tanks. I saw limbs scattered across the road and rebels yelling, "Allahu Akbar." I also saw religious funerals of fallen fighters and rebel camps in the mountains. The images were horrendous. But I learned something about their way of life.

Tajik: "Every rebel group tries to record their actions with just the same camera as we have."

New Year's Eve was about to knock on the door. The Russian saying: "how you meet the new year, that is what you will do the rest of the year," came to fruition last year. Another year as a hostage would be very tough.

Chapter 18
Questioning My Captors

Early in the morning, I woke up from the cold. The heater did not work. I usually saw the elements glow red in the dark. But now the room was pitch black. It looked like a power failure.

It was hard to get used to the cold. I saw my breath in the candlelight and put on some extra clothes. I met New Year's Day in the cold. I hoped it would not be such a cold winter like last year.

We were in the cold and the dark for two days. We used the few available candles only during cooking and washing. Time passed by very slowly. I only got out of bed for the most necessary things.

Tajik decided to surpass the electricity meter illegally.

Me: "Does the power company check for illegal tapping?"

To be in trouble just because we needed electricity did not seem to be a good reason

Tajik: "No, don't worry; they won't notice."

Professor and Tajik did not worry about it.

Tajik left to buy some things to restore the power and asked if I wanted an alcohol-free beer. I used to like a beer, but I asked him to bring a Mars candy bar instead. I ate it bit by bit, and it lasted for two days.

Professor read a lot, and Tajik and I watched a lot of TV. It was incredibly stimulating to follow the news. Sometimes there was news from the Netherlands.

Another two weeks passed. My patience was running out. The lack of news annoyed me. Did General deliver the video? Did my father know anyone in Dagestan who was helping him get me free? I would like to have more details. I hoped General would start the negotiations himself. Whoever had worked on my case could not look back at any significant successes.

The days went by almost unnoticed in their slow rhythm. It was still too early to worry about possible new negotiations. I had a roof over my head, and I ate good food. My physical health remained reasonable, and emotionally I could keep it up for a while. Since General had taken a personal interest in the negotiations, I was hopeful.

After ten days, Povar and Armen replaced Professor and Tajik. I was not excited about that. They were not a paragon of mental stability. I would have felt better if one stable guard stayed with me.

Armen was the leader of the two. He was much more careful than the others and did not want us to make any noise. Cautious from experience or fear, I did not know.

We lowered the volume of the TV. When Armen heard the slightest unrecognizable sound, he turned the sound off altogether. He stood up, grabbed his gun, and listened. When it turned out to be a false alarm, he paced back and forth. Finally, he sat down again on the edge of the couch.

His behavior reminded me of a conversation I had with some of the guards before. Many Russian soldiers suffered from Chechen syndrome, also known as Afghan syndrome. The syndrome was the Russian term for war traumas.

Professor, Tank, Tajik, and Peak wholeheartedly believed that Muslim rebels were spiritually superior to the Russians. They did not need alcohol and drugs before going into a fight. Also, war traumas did not affect them.

Armen: "Only the support of God can explain the differences."

Me: "You may be less bothered by it because you are the defending party who knows the terrain better. Rebel fighters often lured Russians into ambushes. You can often prepare your actions better, and so you know more what to expect. Trust and faith in God and your cause plays a role.

Russian soldiers fight on assignment and often against their own will."

Armen: "Yes, that's why they drink so much and use drugs."

Me: "Not just Russian, rebels, too; I read plenty of stories."

Armen: "Rebels used to rely on drugs, but since the second war in 1999, all bandit rebels have stopped. It became too dangerous for them. Or they may have become true Muslim fighters who obey religious laws. Everyone knows that real Muslims do not lower themselves like that."

I had my doubts about their mental immunity towards war trauma. Not all rebels were as stable and unaffected as they wanted me to believe. However, the revolutionaries disagreed with me.

Armen: "That's the way we are. It is not because of the struggle."

They used trauma to explain Tank's introverted behavior and Povar's hot temper. Also, General got emotional and angry during his stories about the fight in Grozny. When I asked if they had nightmares or flashbacks, they did not want to comment.

As I expected, Povar and Armen adjusted their schedule to their TV programs and stayed up late. It did not take long before I received conflicting commands. I could wash, but according to Armen, there was not enough water to wash clothes. Later

Povar told me to wash my clothes but to hurry up. I quickly started to wash my socks and underwear. Then Armen came in to clean himself for the afternoon prayer.

Armen: "I told you not to wash. Why are you doing that?"

The foam of exasperation almost oozed out of his mouth.

Me: "Povar allowed me to wash quickly."

Armen: "He did not say that."

Me: "Ask him yourself."

Armen: "You have to listen to me and not do what you want."

Me: "When I hear two conflicting commands, I choose what suits me best. Professor and Tajik were not so difficult with the water."

Armen: "I am the one who gets the water."

Me: "You are less clean than I expected. General told us to share fairly."

Armen: "He is not there now, and you will have to deal with me."

Povar intervened and told Armen that he said I could wash my underwear quickly. In the evening, while watching television, Armen came back to the washing incident.

Armen: "You only try to pick out the good things here for yourself. For us, it is not normal that we have to look after you for so long."

Me: "I almost feel sorry for you. You should not think so black and white. There are more colors."

Luckily, contact with Povar was better. When he was on duty, we almost always cooked together. He liked to give orders that I followed with a bit of sass. He came to my room a lot to combat his boredom and to provide me with some encouragement. He asked for advice on weight loss and on how to work on his abs. He noticed that my training regimen was bearing fruit.

The movie Heat with Al Pacino and Robert de Niro played on television, and Povar and I stayed up to watch. Armen had already fallen asleep. During the commercial Povar channel surfed to Playboy Late Night. Armen would have changed the channel. I liked it for a short while, but I preferred to watch the movie. That was not because I was so stuffy, but to view bare breasts with a Muslim fanatic was the other extreme. The fact that he was sitting with his hands under the bed cover made it all a bit uncomfortable.

One day Armen asked me to help him with his boxing skills. It was funny to see how rumors grow into truths. I did not want to train with him, but I realized that it was better for our association. After all, he was wearing a mask against his will when I watched TV. He punched like a farmer with a lot of strength. Slowly I shared my knowledge with him.

The three of us were watching TV, and Armen had fallen asleep again. Suddenly he woke up from a dream, took off his mask, and looked around nervously.

Armen: "What is going on?!"

Povar and I looked at him in surprise. I turned my face away and held my hand to the left of my face to signal that I did not see anything.

Armen: "Have you seen my face? Baltimor, have you seen my face?"

Me: "I've just seen the side of your face."

Armen: "You could have looked away."

Povar: "Yes, you could have looked away. Armen, why do you act so strange? Nothing is going on here. Why do you take off your mask? How could Baltimor not see it?" Povar laughed, and Armen relaxed a bit.

Armen: "Did I look good?"

Me: "I couldn't see with your beard."

Armen continued to sulk, walked back and forth, and ate something in the kitchen. He came back to chat.

I told him a story that I heard from General.

"Once upon a time, there was a warrior, a faithful companion of Muhammed. He engaged in a war for years against an army led by a Persian leader. After years of warring, the two warriors faced each other on the battlefield. Muhammad's henchman raised his sword to behead the Persian. 'There is no God but Allah, and Muhammad is his last prophet,' yells the Persian leader. But the faithful companion of Muhammad killed him anyway."

At home in Medina, instead of being honored, Muhammad wants to sentence him to death.

Companion: "But why, Muhammed?"

Muhammad: "You just killed a fellow Muslim."

Companion: "Yes, but he is not a Muslim. He only called that to save his ass."

Muhammad: "Are you God?"

Companion: "No, no, far from it."

Muhammad: "Then you have to leave these kinds of decisions to God and not yourself."

Armen had been listening carefully.

Armen: "You are not a Muslim, are you?"

Me: "No, but it is just an example to show that it is better to let God judge than yourself."

Armen: "Like you know the Quran better than I do."

Me: "No, but I am more open-minded than you."

It was already a month since the last video. My unrest was increasing. I still did not know if General got involved in the negotiations.

Povar: "I'm just going to help Armen with cooking. Stay calm."

Povar walked towards the kitchen. I was sitting alone in the living room, and suddenly I noticed Armen's gun lying on the couch. It was two steps away.

The guards were unarmed in the kitchen. All I had to do was grab the gun, walk to the kitchen, shoot them, and I was free. But could I escape for sure? What was outside? Where did I have to go? Are there more henchmen? Would I be able to kill Povar and Armen? Did I want to kill them?

I had plenty of time to think about all these questions. The gun had an enormous appeal. My release would happen soon. A bit pointless to shoot them now.

Did I want the death of two people on my conscience? I did not care about Armen, but if I shoot him, I must kill Povar. What was the best thing to do now? If they had to kill me, they would do it. There was an afternoon program for women on TV. The gun was remarkably close. Armen always loaded his gun after practicing.

I turned my head several times from the TV to the couch and back to the TV. It was quiet in the kitchen. Did they know I controlled their destiny? If I wanted to shoot them, I had better do it rapidly.

I felt glued to my seat. I heard someone walking back.

Povar: "Are you still here?"

Me: "Yes, what should I have done?"

Povar: "Why didn't you shoot us?"

Me: "You have behaved too kindly. We have become too close. Besides, God forbids us to kill without reason."

Povar: "You are not as religious as we are?"

Me: "No, but in my way, I am religious."

Povar: "Yes, I made a mistake. You should go to your room when I walk out of here."

For hours I mulled over whether I acted in the right way. I decided that if I got another opportunity, I would tie them up and then walk away. There was enough tape, rope, and I could lock the doors.

Professor arrived in the night between 29 to 30 January, and Povar packed his things in the morning and was happy to leave. He gave me his aftershave and deodorant.

I heard a lot of talking late in the afternoon; the men were restless. I had not left my room all day, and Professor came into my room for a chat. I told him about the gun incident.

Professor: "I think this is the last time you can control yourself."

Me: "It is better not to leave anything lying around. Have you heard anything from General?"

Professor: "No, I haven't seen him in a while."

Professor had to leave, and moments later, Armen entered my room .

Armen: "Baltimor, we're moving. Pack your things quickly, and leave all the books here. We'll bring them tomorrow."

Me: "Where are we going?"

Armen: "You will like the place where we are going."

Me: "To the big house?"

Armen: "Maybe."

The move seemed riskier this time, hasty, and unplanned. The men were incredibly quiet.

Armen: "Are you tense? That is not needed; everything will be fine."

I sat in the cold on my wooden chair because we already packed the heater. I secretly packed one book. At least I had something to do before the TV, and other books arrived.

I saw General in the car. Everyone was tense. I had time to ask questions later at the other house. Once again, I sat blindfolded in the back seat. I took a deep breath to relax and did not show my fear. If the police stopped us, it would be a tragic end. I heard the boys breathing quietly. Did they have everything under control? It was hot in the car, and we were squeezed together on the narrow back seat. I got nauseous due to the heat.

Me: "Can you switch off the heater? Otherwise, things will not go well here."

General drove and turned down the heater. Fortunately, the journey went well, and soon I was in the same room as six weeks ago. My things were already there, but there was no water, toilet, or basin. I saw the massive barbell and some smaller new barbells.

The room had changed. Someone renovated it into a storage room for old junk. Till deep in the night, I organized the space. I moved lots of trash and found my hidden antenna. If I stayed here until my release, I would be satisfied.

In the morning, nobody came with food. I did not hear anyone. Maybe the whole house was empty. I had an "Emergency Go Kit" with me. I had a bottle of water, a bottle for my urine, and some dry bread. I would not starve, but where to go to the toilet? And how could I wash? One bottle of water was not much.

I did some weightlifting, which took me more effort than six weeks ago. I repaired the old wooden chair with a hammer, some nails, and a plastic rope. The repair made noise, but nobody came to tell me to be quiet. So, I was alone.

I was happy with my book and had time to read. I waited for the arrival of the rebels and the television, but it remained deadly quiet. When no one came by in the evening, I worried. Were they arrested? We left so mysteriously and quickly. General did not have time to share the latest news.

Unfortunately, it was impossible to escape from this cellar. Would I die of hunger and thirst here?

Chapter 19
Hope Brought Life

The following morning, I concentrated on weightlifting. Even though I was utterly alone, I liked it better here. This living space gave me a degree of independence that made up for a lot. Because I had no safe water, I did not brush my teeth. Would the guys reveal my location if they got arrested? For more than a day and a half, I had not heard anyone except the sound of the imam.

My incarceration had lasted for almost a year and a half. Unbelievable from which reserves people can draw strength under extreme circumstances. Except for two days of diarrhea, I had never been sick. I never had a fever and never had a cold. My bowels felt uncomfortable, probably related to stress. I had always been able to control my aggression and emotions when necessary. I had dealt with the guards, and I learned patience. I continued to eat and maintained my hygiene. Many hostages neglected themselves after long periods of imprisonment.

Months ago, I imagined that the abduction would have been more straightforward. Had I known my captivity would last at least eighteen months, I probably would not have made it. Hope brought life; it did.

I did not know what situation in daily life that was comparable to this nightmare. After my release, could I explain how I felt and what I experienced? There were words for it, but I did not have them.

It was interesting to notice how my memory dealt with these hardships. The days went by slowly, but strangely some periods passed by quickly. I had been a hostage for 536 days. I counted every day and night more than once but looking back now, it seemed much less. Was this because I experienced so little every day?

Last year's winter was cold when I was in the middle of it. Sometimes it felt like I almost froze to death, but I told myself that it was not bad. Although, in hindsight, the time seemed shorter and the circumstances less severe. It was better not to think of another period of 536 days with four months of cold. I longed for my freedom, but I tried not to think about it too much. By reading and training, I shut my mind off from the outside world. The longer it took, the more frustrating it became. My detention remained a waste of my time. I only had one life and wanted it to be useful. I still had so much to do. If those working on my release also made quality use of their time on my behalf, I might go home soon.

Early in the evening, I heard women's voices outside. Moments later, Armen came in with sausage, bread, and a bottle of lemonade. Armen insisted he filled my bottle with water. Russian soldiers of the police did not arrest the men. I would not starve, and I did not gain my freedom.

Monday evening, 2 February, the birthday of my youngest brother, we moved again.

General: "The owner wants to continue with his renovation."

I reluctantly collected my things and waited for what was to come.

Me: "Can I bring those little dumbbells?"

General: "Yes, that is good."

Me: "Can I have a glass of water?"

General gave me a glass of water, and I gulped it down.

In the car, it was less tense than three days ago.

We drove for only about 30 minutes.

General: "Get out quickly; get out quickly."

Tajik carried me on his back down a slope, and we entered a house. Povar grabbed my hand, and we carefully walked further.

Povar: "Sit on your mattress and stay calm."

I was curious about how this room looked. I smelled mold and sat against a damp wall. Povar tried to turn on the electricity. After half an hour, I could take off my blindfold. Three pieces of old, greasy, orange-brown linoleum and long hair covered the floor. Damp, moldy wallpaper peeled off the walls.

Povar: "What do you think about it?"

Me: "It is okay."

Povar: "Do not be so picky."

The room had a high ceiling. There was a small window with an insect screen, allowing a little daylight to come through. Maybe I could escape through the small window later. Next to the door was a cheap bathroom cabinet with a mirror, a coat rack, and a small cupboard on the room's left side. The cabinet contained make-up, soap, deodorant, and a bag with dark brown hair. There was a calendar on the wall.

The door to the room where Armen and Povar stayed could not close due to the extension cord. Through the frosted glass, I could see their silhouettes. The decrepit house had a dismal appearance. Even the men did not like the place. We had been there for a few days, and I had not left my room yet. Armen was in the house regularly. Kasparov and Povar alternated. Due to supply problems, there was not much to eat. The days turned monotonous. No one cooked anymore.

Most of the time, I ate bread with sausages. Occasionally we ate lukewarm black bean soup or a small piece of roast chicken.

Hygiene conditions had never been this bad. Again, they chose a house without a water supply. Maybe the whole village was without running water. This time there was even less water than in recent weeks. In the evening, I had to ask for water to wash. They filled two plastic jugs that can hold two liters of water.

Armen: "Don't use it all at once."

Since January 22, I did not have enough water for a full-body wash. I managed to wash my intimate parts every day and my armpits every other day.

Again, I could only go to the toilet in the evening. Through the living room, kitchen, and across the yard, the guard led me to an old derelict barn. The wooden toilet seat stood next to a 3-foot-high pile of excrement. A high heap was already forming under the toilet. Someone would have to move the bathroom again soon.

The bathroom of the previous residents was in the same piggery. We did not use it. I knew that many people in Dagestan had to make ends meet with little money, but I had never seen this poverty level.

Me: "How can a person live in this dump?"

251

Povar: "It often has to do with a family's lack of financial resources."

Me: "Do not the women in the family complain?"

Povar: "Maybe they are not used to anything better."

Me: "Don't your women run away without a normal bathroom and toilet."

Povar: "Is it that important?"

The boredom increased. The men had some structure because of their prayers. Fortunately, I slept more than ever. There was no chair, so I hardly got off my bed. I usually read with my back to the wall. I was still reading the same book since we moved at the end of January. Altogether I had read it ten times by now. I was angry at myself for not bringing more books.

Povar occasionally came over for a chat. In the evening, we worked out together. He took a chair and a large mirror from their room to see our progress, just like in the gym. If Povar was not there, I lost my focus on doing my exercises.

Filthy living conditions made it hard to maintain a positive attitude. The call to prayer from the mosque also started to get on my nerves. I heard two imams sing five times a day. I wondered who got more visitors to their mosque. I guessed the imam with the best voice.

My potential escape window worked like a carrot hanging on a stick for a horse. I fantasized about which route to follow to get home. Unfortunately, the window was too high. I had no way to climb and work my way up to the window. I put the dumbbells against the wall. I was still not high enough. Under the pressure of my weight, the dumbbells made deep marks in the wallpaper. I put the two dumbbells together and stood on them. Balancing was not easy, but it worked. Nervous excitement ran through my body. If the guards caught me, they would not respond in a friendly way. If I managed to escape, they were the ones to be punished.

It was impossible to remove the iron insect screen. I managed to look outside, but it did not make me any wiser. I saw the neighbor's house and the mountainous terrain. I could escape unnoticed if not for the metal screen. I felt disappointed, but maybe there was a better way.

It was becoming increasingly difficult to remain positive. I had nothing to do, and I got deeper and deeper into myself. After three weeks without a good wash, my beard irritated my face. When I scratched my beard, flakes of skin fell out. I knew the rebels did not want me to cut my beard, but I decided to shorten my beard with some disposable razor blades.

Armen: "General told you not to shave because we may need to record a video."

Povar and Kasparov complimented me on how I looked better with a short beard.

Me: "General promised to come with some news soon. Two months have passed, and I have not heard anything. Why should I stick to my agreements? You guys can't even plan a ransom payment or a prisoner exchange."

Armen: "If you want, we will have it solved in no time. We will just shoot you. Do you want it that way?"

Me: "I would rather not but sitting here wasting time does not make sense either. Do you know if General made contact? Why should I ask you anyway? You always act like you do not know anything. Why can't you tell me? Why do you always have to be so suspicious?"

Armen: "You have to deal with me now. I want you to listen to me."

Me: "When it comes to shaving, it is already too late. With so little water, I could not keep it clean. Do you wash properly, or do you just spray some deodorant without washing?"

Armen came to my room occasionally to put on some deodorant I got from Povar. I have reached a point where I did not care anymore. My hope for a quick settlement had vanished. Armen came back a little later.

Armen: "Baltimor, stay calm. No one envies you, but it is not normal for you to get mad with me like that. You do not realize how well we treat you here."

Me: "It is not that good anymore nowadays. It would be better to go back to the first house.

Armen: "Don't count on returning there. Come on, hold on."

Me: "I will do my best."

Fortunately, Povar brought me a magazine about cars with all the latest models. I read the tests ranging from Ferrari's and Porsches to Fords and Renaults. I imagined driving in the most beautiful convertibles. I cruised along boulevards and beaches. Povar and I chose our favorites. He liked the Ferrari, and I wanted the Porsche 911 GT.

A Mars or Snickers candy, a friendly word from Tajik, or Povar coming over to read made me feel better.

The men did not talk much, and it became increasingly quiet at home. No one liked this place. To the relief of everyone, we moved again in mid-February. The move went smoothly. The guards packed everything very fast, and we were on our way in no time. It was the shortest journey so far. I no longer experienced tension when moving.

The first impression of my new room was okay, although it was filthy. I felt incredibly happy with a large soft chair. By hostage standards, I had a comfortable bed. My room had two bedside tables and a large wardrobe with two mirrors. The linoleum and wallpaper looked better than in the previous house.

The guards slept in the room next to mine. My door had a large lock, and an old cloth covered the window. I liked the cloth curtain because the men cannot peek in or come in unexpectedly. I still heard the two imams calling for prayer.

I had a bucket full of water, although I did not know how long it should last. A couple of new books and I would be acceptable to hold on. Maybe I could even wash my clothes. I had not rinsed my clothes since the beginning of this year. My shirt and underpants started to fall apart. I had worn them for 18 months in a row. They were threadbare, and I could see through them. The elastic in my boxer shorts wore out, and I folded them around my training pants to hold them in place.

I could not get a good wash here either. The amount of water was again limited.

I brought the dumbbells with me, and I did my exercises every day. Reading in my lazy chair was a lot more pleasant than before, even though I knew the car magazine and book by heart now.

The food was good. There was often chicken soup, plov, and ginkal. Ginkal is a dish of cooked, sticky dough cut into squares with dried or roasted meat in a sauce. The first time I smelled the dried meat, I thought it was spoiled, but gradually I started to like it.

Due to my privacy and access to a mirror, I could no longer suppress the urge to masturbate. The discharge was pleasant after such a long time. Maybe I should have done it earlier. It would be marvelous to have sex again! One of my books was about a man who was in prison for a long time. When finally released, women felt a great attraction to him. It seemed that women had a great interest in knowing that a man had not been with a woman for a long time. They expected a beast in bed. I was curious about how it would go when I returned. Sadness accompanied my sexual relief. I wanted to experience real love again.

The boredom was so great that my thoughts made me bored. A new book would be a good boost. I asked them several times to buy a new book, but somehow, they could not find a bookstore.

Armen's behavior got on my nerves. The others put on their masks when they came in. He always ordered me to turn around. Reluctantly I obeyed. He did not return the borrowed dumbbells or deodorant without me asking. The men had a television, but they did not invite me to watch it with them. I felt excluded.

It was dinner time, and I heard Armen unlocking the door.

Armen: *"Ot vernish!* Turn around!"

Me: "No. I don't feel like turning around anymore."

Armen: "Have you turned around yet?"

Me: "No, I am not going to turn around."

Armen: "Turn around! What do you think you are doing?"

Me: "Put on your mask."

Armen: "Turn around; you are playing with fire."

Me: "No, just put on your mask."

Armen: "If I enter and you see my face, I will have to shoot you. So better turn around!"

Me: "Are you deaf?"

He closed the door, and a bit later, he entered the room. He breathed heavily through his mask. He had his gun pointed towards the ground. I could no longer control myself.

Me: "You are a hero with your gun. You don't dare do it with your hands."

Armen: "I don't need that gun."

Me: "Then put it away and come on."

I sat quietly in my chair and felt calm. I did not care what happened anymore.

Armen: "Be smart, Baltimor, because I will hit you."

Me: "Don't be so sure. I am ready to beat you up."

Armen did not know what to do. I crossed the line, but I did not want to be the first to give in.

Tajik entered the room, and although he said nothing, he had a de-escalating presence.

Armen: "What are you doing now? Do you know how dangerous you make it for everyone? Do you have something against me? Why you always take it out on me?"

Me: "When I am in a bad mood, your behavior works like a red rag in front of a bull. Today is such a bad day. You have just had bad luck twice."

I did not want to hurt his feelings. I did not want to come across as someone who complained about his behavior.

Armen: "I would have preferred you to be gone by now, but I can't do much about it, either."

Me: "Let us forget about it. I will try to restrain myself."

Professor arrived one day later. I had not seen him since the end of January and was delighted with his visit. We caught up and discussed yesterday's incident.

Professor: "General asks you to stay strong for a while longer. He is busy with your case. There may be news soon."

Me: "I just have nothing left to do. I only have one book that I read five times in a row."

Professor: "Where is the rest of them?"

Me: "I was not allowed to take them when we suddenly moved four weeks ago. Can General arrange new books?"

Professor: "I'll pass it on to him."

He gave me a bucket full of water and left again.

Chapter 20
New News

On March 2, I heard Professor in the room next to me. I expected him to come at any time, but I was disappointed. Was he abandoning me too? Povar was the only one who came to chat. Povar with whom I had such a complicated relationship during the first ten months.

A few hours later, Professor came in. He sat down on the bed and started to leaf through the car magazine.

Professor: "For how long did you not drive a car?"

Me: "Counting those four months before my abduction, 23 months in total."

Professor: "You can drive yourself again in three months."

Me: "What do you mean?"

Professor: "We made another contact, and if everything goes well, you will be home at the end of May."

Professor was curious about my reaction and looked at me inquisitively.

Finally, I received the news! I was enjoying it. For the first time in a few weeks, I could smile again. I needed this.

Me: "What is going on? Is General doing the negotiations himself? Did he go abroad?"

Professor did not know the answers or did not want to give them. It did not matter, and I set my new end date in 90 days at the end of May. Three months ago, I was still in the big house. How many relocations had there been? Time flies so fast.

On March 6, I missed my mother's birthday for the second time. She turned sixty-five. In two months, I would have missed all the birthdays twice. At the end of 2004, my parents would be married for forty years. Then I had to be back. Birthdays, Christmas, and New Year's Eve were the days when we all met. Would I ever see them again? The reason I endured all this time had to do with my will to be with my family. I would not abandon my family. They expected me to come back, and I will go back home to them.

Tajik gave me a new book, and my dark thoughts disappeared. The book was about the same agent Drongo which I had seen in one of the series I watched. As usual, I read the book slowly.

The relationship with Armen had returned to normal. I did my best to chit chat.

Armen: "By the way, you can also watch TV here again soon."

Me: "That is a nice surprise."

Armen: "Tomorrow, I will go to the supermarket. Is there anything I can bring you to make your stay more enjoyable?"

What a fantastic choice; I missed so many things such as peanut butter, chocolate, beer, or a simple slice of pizza. I lost more than 40 pounds.

Me: "If you can bring me a can of Coca-Cola, that would be wonderful. I have not had that in nineteen months."

The next day I was looking forward to my first coke in months. When Armen opened the door, I got a can of Pepsi-light. Not precisely as I wished, but it was still nice that he granted my request.

A day before my birthday, Professor came again.

Me: "Tomorrow is my birthday. Already the second year that I cannot celebrate. It would be so nice to have something sweet."

Professor: "At home, you can eat something sweet. You know we do not celebrate birthdays."

Me: "But we do."

Professor: "Do you usually celebrate it with your family?"

I explained to him how we celebrated birthdays in the Netherlands. I went to bed full of expectations.

Would one of the guards buy me a present? My hope was in vain because the guards did not purchase anything for me. I felt a bit disappointed and read my book. In the evening, Kasparov came with a bag full of small sweets, fruit, and a Mars candy bar.

Kasparov: "Baltimor, congratulations. I hope you will celebrate your next birthday at home. Then we will finally get rid of you."

Me: "Thank you, nice that you thought of me. I appreciate it."

Kasparov: "You are not a bad guy, either."

The days after my birthday, I slowly ate my sweets and fruit. I was a bit proud of myself. After all, it was rare that abductors bought presents for the hostage's birthdays.

I decided to walk through my room more often than before. Occasionally I stood still by the door to listen to the television. I heard about a bomb attack in Madrid.

Me: "What happened?"

Armen: "Muslim terrorists have blown up a train station, with hundreds of deaths and thousands wounded."

I remembered Professor's words that jihad would only end when Spain turned Islamic.

My three new books arrived in mid-March. I had to read them three times, and then I could go home. The books helped me to withdraw from my small world.

Me: "Are we staying in this house until the end?"

Armen: "I think so, but anything can still happen."

Armen finally gave a regular answer to one of my questions, although he appeared to be wrong. On March 15, the guards received a signal that we had to move again. We left late at night. Blindfolded, they led me outside. General was waiting for me next to the car.

General: "It will be a long drive. Sorry, but you must get into the trunk. It is larger than before."

We left for the new house. We reached our destination, and I exited the trunk of the car.

General: "Take off your blindfold. I have a surprise for you."

Curious about my new environment, I followed the instructions of General. To my utter surprise, we were once again at the gravel excavation, the same place where General collected me nineteen months ago.

General: "I told you that we would not return after this, but hey, this is how Allah wants it."

Me: "Back to my first room. Will we stay there until the release?"

General: "That is the intention. Do you like the idea?"

It seemed like a perfect option. Everyone here knew what to expect from each other. We had spent fourteen months in this house without significant problems, and the next 75 days should be fine as well. We had enough water, and even the cursed toilet was better than anything I had seen in the last three months. Maybe I could sit outside in the sun again.

General: "If you put your blindfold on, we will start hiking. Did you stay fit all these months?"

Me: "I'll manage this trip."

I thought it was a shame that I had to put on my blindfold. I had not been outside since October. Povar, Armen, Tajik, Professor, and I walked into the mountains. Because of my blindfold, we moved slow, and Tajik removed my blindfold.

Tajik: "Don't look back."

Me: "Do not worry, I am so happy that I can walk outside again; I will not spoil the moment."

It was terrific to inhale the fresh winter air. I smelled the pine trees and the raw dong of cows. I saw the last scraps of snow that were still lying here and there behind rocks. The moon's natural glow lit the small trails made by residents, cattle, and the sporadic car. Higher up in the mountains, we turned off the road and walked over a mountain top. It was all so similar here that I could never have found my way back.

Tajik: "Look at the ground; look at the ground!"

We slowly descended until we were close to a small country road. Here we stopped for a moment and waited for two guards. After fifteen minutes, they arrived and reported that everything was under control. They blindfolded me again, and we walked along the trail to the hideout.

The break of dawn set in, and it got lighter. I felt exhausted but also safe. It even felt a bit like home!

Povar: "Three more weeks, and then you're out of here."

I was surprised because they first told me at the end of May. I decided just to ignore his comment.

The hiding place had probably been vacant. My room was full of cobwebs, and it was damp and cold. The transition to dusk and cold was jarring after five months of heating and light. The first night I could not sleep because of the cold.

The next day was a cleaning day. I scrubbed the floor and removed the mold from the walls and ceiling. The stale air made way for fresh mountain air. From the outside, I heard the birds singing; spring was knocking on the door. The war on insects started; their easy life was over! I would take my territory back.

Professor and Armen guarded me. The old rhythm did not fully return. There was less water than before, and I was not allowed to go outside at night.

Professor invited me to sit in the kitchen again. We had conversations about religion, politics, history, and geography as before. Armen occasionally joined us but usually kept aloof. During the daytime, I read my new books. I had nothing else to do.

With only two more months to go, thoughts of my home occupied my mind more often than before. The reunion with my family would be close and warm. My mother would be the one most relieved. How many times did she tell me to come back and live and work in the Netherlands again? My father was proud of me and the work I did, but he had always told me to be careful. Maybe we could all go on a skiing holiday again. Those used to be fantastic holidays!

I imagined my release and fantasized about how I would meet my soccer team. When I unexpectedly step on the field, my friend Olaf would notice me, pick up the ball, and, together with the team, would run to me. Even the opposing team and referee would join the celebration.

It would be nice to go on an ice bear camp between Christmas and New Year with my friends from Rotterdam. We called Ice Bear Camp our camping time with lots of mud, barbecue, and drinks to greet the end of the year.

Professor encouraged me not to fall into my old sins anymore.

Professor: "Stop drinking. Get married; you are already thirty-four. You think you must live a good life on earth. Your destination should be a heaven where you can live in luxury forever."

Me: "I first have to catch up and celebrate freedom, then I'll see if I can improve my life."

Professor: "Arjan Dirkowitsj, Arjan Dirkowitsj Erkel. Soon it will be too late. You will have an accident, and you will end up in hell for the rest of your life."

The days were ticking by. My mood was generally quite good. Sixty days till the end of May seemed an extraordinarily little time, especially if I told myself that I would be back in Rotterdam in less than two months.

It sounded much worse when I imagined that I had to sit in this small, dark room for almost nine weeks. At that moment, my room corresponded to a porch of death. It was so dim that it seemed as if the world of the living had already said goodbye to me.

Me: "Professor, can you provide some plastic bags?"

I was worried that I would no longer have a toilet.

Professor: "There is good news. You might be released by the end of April. If everything goes well, maybe even by the end of next week."

Me: "Is that what Povar was talking about when we arrived here?"

Professor: "Did he say that? Yes, we knew it. But they told you the end of May so that you would not be disappointed if it did not work out early April."

Me: "So maybe this is the last week?"

Professor: "It could be, but let's focus on the end of May; that is better."

I set a date for myself at the end of April so that I could celebrate Queen's Day at home again. Secretly I hoped the beginning of April

On April 1. they allowed me to go outside during the day for the first time in six months. Professor and I sat in front of the door in the sun. He played with his kalashnikov while we talked. He pointed at a spot in the distance and pretended to shoot.

Me: "Could you live your life without this?"

Professor: "What life?"

Me: "The rebel life?"

Professor: "How do you mean?"

Me: "A large part of your motivation has to do with religion or independence. But also, with the romance of rebel existence."

Professor: "Romance? Being hunted down, lack of comfort, excitement, and death. It does not sound romantic."

He thinks a little more.

Professor: "Yes, you are right. Yes, it is romantic. There is companionship, freedom, struggle, joy, and faith. It will be difficult to return to a normal life. I probably cannot live without it anymore."

Me: "What will you do if the war ends here?"

Professor: "The holy war continues. I will continue to fight until Spain is Islamic. The first attacks are already there."

I saw from the eyes and corners of his mouth that he was smiling.

The first week of April passed without news. The end of the month was still far away; I was not worried yet. The worst cold was over, and there was more water. For the first time in a long time, I had enough water for a good wash. I could finally wash my underwear. It made me feel better.

On Friday, April 9, Armen woke me up in the middle of the night.

Armen: "Get dressed quickly; we have to go down to the valley."

Me: "Must I pack my things?"

Armen: "No, that is not necessary."

I wanted to wait for Professor to make sure they did not allow me to take anything. I did not want to be without books again.

Professor: "No, General told us to hurry up. I do not know why."

Me: "Can I take my toothbrush and toothpaste?"

Professor: "If it fits in your pockets, take it with you."

All sorts of weird thoughts went through my mind. What was going to happen? Were they going to kill me after all? Had the negotiation process been terminated? How were we going to walk down? Professor remained calm, but could Armen control himself?

I quickly used some deodorant to hide my cold sweat. It was the last bit of what Tank gave me ten months ago. I only used it for special occasions such as birthdays and holidays.

Blindfolded, I walked between Professor and Armen to the valley. It was a sultry spring evening. Professor told me in October that it was easier to kill me here than in the valley. Was this still true? As we walked further down, the negative thoughts gave way to positive ones. The smell of flowers, fresh leaves, and grass tickled my nose. I heard dogs barking, some chickens, and cows. The wind blew softly through my hair, and everything was going to be okay.

Down at the gravel excavation, we waited a few minutes for General and the car. He shook my hand, gave me a Mars candy bar, and told me to sit in the back seat.

I sat between Povar and Tajik. Everyone was dead quiet. I heard the tires hitting the road and the crackling of the rebels' thick, synthetic winter coats. The two-way radios were ringing regularly, and General was getting stressed and upset.

We drove in circles again. After a few hours, General broke the silence.

General: "We wanted to transfer you to another group tonight. They would arrange your release within a few weeks. They did not show up, but tomorrow we will try again."

Me: "Transfer? To another group?"

General: "We will try again tomorrow, and I will explain everything to you. You must go back with the guys now. Make sure you wash all your clothes tomorrow. I do not know how the new group will treat you, but then you will be clean, at least."

Great story, I was being transferred to a new group. General promised to stay with me until the end. I felt insecure and anxious. Would it go wrong after all?

On the way up, I was tired. I was not used to walking a lot.

Professor: "Rest a while. I also need a break. I have not slept well in days, and I have not been training in recent weeks. You must be completely gone."

Me: "Yes, it is a bit too much. Tomorrow we have to descend the whole way again."

I could not sleep because of the tension. What awaited me? What kind of men would they be? Were they disciplined, or would they treat me like cattle?

Armen put on water and called me to the kitchen early to wash and do the laundry.

Armen: "Look, I am heating some water for you."

He happily pointed to a half-full bucket on the stove. I had to restrain myself from asking why he did not fill the bucket.

Armen: "You can wash your clothes here in the sink."

Me: "I prefer to do it as usual in the red tub in the bathroom."

Armen: "This time, you have to use the sink."

Me: "There is no plug for the sink, and it is way too low for me."

Armen: "I want you to do it here."

Me: "Why do you care where I wash? I am not getting in the way there either."

Armen: "You do it here, or you forget about it."

Me: "There is not enough water to wash it all anyway. You are always stingy with water."

Armen: "What did you say?"

Me: "You heard me. You are stingy."

Armen: "What is stingy? I put the water on the gas, especially for you. We can add cold water soon."

Me: "It is just not enough, and I am not going to wash here."

We shouted at each other and were about to fight. Professor ran from the bedroom and stood between us.

Professor: "Do the laundry in the bathroom. With cold water, there is enough water."

Armen: *"Ah ty kozyol,* ah you bastard."

Me: *"Ot kozla slyshna!"* I hear it from a jerk."

Professor: "Go and wash your clothes."

I did the laundry with the door open. Armen came into the kitchen after a while to make peace.

Armen: "I tried to do my best. I heated water, especially for you, so you could wash in the kitchen and not in the shower room that we use as our toilet now."

Me: "Yes, I now realize that, but I wanted to do it the old-fashioned way."

Armen: "Men can have arguments as long as we don't stay angry with each other."

Me: "Friends?" I reached out to him.

Armen: "Friends." He responded to my gesture, and we shook hands.

Armen: "We are both stressed. You want to go home, and we do not want to guard you."

It was a good thing that disciplined guards were holding me. Armen also tried to show his kind side in one way or another. Maybe I was too unkind to him.

In the afternoon, my clothes dried. I felt freshly washed. Professor and I were in the kitchen.

Me: "Professor, thank you for your attention and good care."

Professor: "You're welcome; I'm glad we didn't make it harder for you than necessary."

Me: "I have one more question; please answer it honestly. Did you talk with me so much because you liked it or out of pity?"

Professor: "Sometimes, I did it because I thought it was sad for you to be locked up all the time. But most of the time, I thought it was interesting. And you, did you just want to sit outside, or was it interesting to talk to me?"

Me: "Of course, I enjoyed being out of my room, but it clicked with you. Your attention certainly helped me."

Professor: "I think everyone now respects you. What mattered to me was how you behaved during the recordings for the ultimatum video."

Me: "If I had behaved like a wimp there, it would probably have become much more difficult for me later."

Professor: "Yes, I think so too. Will you ever become a Muslim?"

Me: "I will buy a Quran, but I doubt very much whether I will ever become a Muslim."

Professor: "You are intelligent enough. If you immerse yourself in religions, you will find that Islam is the only true religion."

Me: "At home, I will catch up with my old life first."

Professor: "You also need a bottle in your room at home; otherwise, the transition is too big. For your great need, you have to ask whether the neighbors want to guide you outside with masks."

Me: "I will never miss your toilet."

My last supper consisted of boiled potatoes in the skin with some ketchup and bread. The radio rang late in the evening, and we started the descent again. Luckily, I did not have any muscle ache from the long walk yesterday. Halfway down, we met

Povar. At the gravel excavation, we waited for the car.

Me: "Armen, I know that we did not always get along well. But I still want to thank you for your commitment to making the best of it at the end."

Armen: "I preferred you would have left earlier, but it looks like your release will happen soon."

Povar came to me and wished me a quick release and reminded me not to tell the police or the secret service too much.

Povar: "We have taken good care of you; do not let us down."

Saying goodbye did not hurt in this case. We had known each other for over a year and a half. Despite everything, I developed a good relationship with Povar, Professor, and General. Not that I would miss them, but it would be interesting to meet them again.

General was very talkative in the car.

General: "I have been thinking about our conversation. About what to tell the secret services about our time together. It is up to you. You can tell the secret services whatever you want. You did not find out much anyway. Just do not tell them too much about our first home."

Me: "What is so exciting about that?"

General: "Maybe not much for you, but for us, it is."

Me: "Anything else?"

General: "You can tell our names and the number of people you saw. Do not paint us as heartless rebels because we don't deserve that."

Me: "I will tell them my side of the story. Where am I going?"

General: "I cannot tell you anything about them. I explained to them how we dealt with you and asked if they would treat you the same. You must also behave, of course."

Me: "I do not have much choice."

General: "What did you think of us?"

Me: "If I compare you to everything I have read about abductions, then you are not so bad. I started to respect your way of life, although it still opposes mine. What did you think of me?"

General: "Of course, I can only speak for myself, but I also respect you and the way you have adapted to this situation. I hope that you will find true faith someday. We are almost there. I did my best to get you out of this situation. I am probably more at risk now than you are. I have not seen any money yet."

I did not know how to react.

Me: "General, you tell the men that I am grateful that they have behaved well. I wish you all a long life, but if that for some reason might not happen, then I wish that you may die as martyrs."

General: "I hope you mean it. I will find out later what you told about us in the media."

The car came to a stop, and General and Tajik got out. Povar touched me and gave me a hand.

Povar: "All the best!"

General came to get me. Due to the excitement, I forgot to say goodbye to Professor and stepped out of the car.

General: "It is a short walk to the other car. You must lie down in the trunk again. Do not feel offended because this time, it is a real big one."

Me: "Thank you, General."

General: "Hold on. Just a little while, and you will be a free man again."

General took my hand, and we pressed our cheeks to each other. I crawled into the trunk, and the lid closed. It was indeed a massive trunk. I could almost lie straight, and without any problem, I could turn from one side to the other. The driver got into the car and turned on the radio. I heard pop music, which meant that I was in the hands of another group. They were not fundamental Muslims.

The car moved fast on well-maintained roads, and the car seemed stable on the road. I had no idea what brand it was. Occasionally the driver slowed down, and the window opened. Probably to pass some police block posts. Did they have the guts to stay on the main roads, or did they have a special pass protecting them from any searches? After driving around for a couple of hours, we arrived in a village. I heard dogs bark, and the roads were getting worse. The car stopped. The doors opened, and I felt the vehicle rise slightly. The men got out, and I heard footsteps and muffled men's voices. They opened the trunk.

One of the men commanded, "Arjan, get out!"

I did as commanded, and one man held me slightly. It was not cold outside, and I saw some light through my blindfold.

The man asked, "Your name is Arjan, right?"

Me: "Yes, Arjan."

The man commanded, "Come and follow us."

We entered a house at a rapid pace as the men guided me up the stairs. It must be a big house. They sat me on a chair, and then it became quiet. I wondered how the place looked. Was there a bed, a bathroom, a couch, a television this time?

The man commanded again, "Take off your blindfold."

The first thing I saw was two faces. I saw one skinny guy with a face like a mug shot and one friendly face. I was shocked because they did not wear masks. I did not dare look them in the eye.

"*Spiyezdom,* Welcome home."

Did they mean that I must feel at home because it might take time before my release?

Chapter 21
The Man in the Picture

Me: "Welcome home?!"

FSB: "Yes, welcome home. You are free."

Me: "Free?" Are they trying to fool me?

FSB: "Yes, you are free. Congratulations!"

I did not want to believe it yet and looked around. It was nothing like a bedroom or a prison. There were several chairs, a computer, and two desks with stacks of paper on it.

FSB: "You are Arjan Erkel, right?"

Me: "Yes."

FSB: "Are you sure? You do not look like the guy in the picture we have of you."

One of the men got up and shuffled through a newspaper.

FSB: "I'm just looking for a picture of you to compare."

Me: "Don't bother; I have my passport with me."

FSB: "Really? Let me see."

I could not convince them that they had the right person in front of them. Someone came to verify my passport.   Due to his age and the way he commanded, I guessed he had a higher rank.

Me: "Am I really free?"

FSB: "Yes, really. Don't you believe us?"

I smiled, but I still did not believe it. I did not indulge in a happy dance.

Me: "It is too good to believe."

FSB: "How are you? You have changed a lot."

Me: "It's really me. In case you want to send me back later."

FSB: "No, we believe you. How was it there? Who detained you?"

The guards warned me that the FSB would probably subject me to a lengthy interrogation. Now I must make sure that I would tell the same story.

FSB: "Were they Chechens?"

Me: "I do not know. The rebels said so."

FSB: "Have you been treated well?   Did they feed you normally? You're so skinny."

Me: "That was up to me. Occasionally I did not eat to relieve my stomach cramps."

FSB: "Where did you learn to speak Russian?"

Me: "In Tajikistan, I used to work there."

I tried to take over the conversation. The men retook control and asked more questions. But they wanted answers to simple queries, and it did not feel like a real interrogation.

Me: "Where am I exactly?"

FSB: "In Makhachkala."

Me: "Oh, by what kind of department?"

FSB: "We can't say that."

Me: "FSB?"

FSB: "Alright, then we set you free with a special unit."

Me: "With a special operation? I did not hear a shot."

FSB: "A special operation does not necessarily mean that we have freed you by force. We have arranged everything so that you are released."

Two Russians walked into the room: one big sweaty, tense guy and a cheerful man with a relaxed attitude. I was still on my guard and waited quietly.

FSB: "Congratulations! How is it going? You must have lived in hell. Bastards."

The cheerful man tried to make eye contact pleasantly.

The sweaty man introduced himself as Sergey. He worked for a society of KGB veterans who took care of my release. He sat down at one of the desks and started making calls on his cell phone. Sweat gushed from his forehead.

Sergey: "Aren't you happy?"

Me: "Of course, I am, but it's all so unexpected. Can I have a glass of water?"

Sergey: "We also have vodka."

Me: "No, thanks."

Sergey: "Are you all right?"

Me: "Because I don't drink? I have some intestine problems, but in general, I am doing fine."

Sergey: "We will soon go to a hotel where you can have a nice bath. You probably have not done that for a long time."

Sergey hands me the phone and whispers, "The Dutch Embassy."

Me: "This is Arjan."

Dutch Diplomat: "Is it really you? How is it going?"

The diplomat introduced himself, but I immediately forgot his name. It started to dawn on me that I was free.

Dutch Diplomat: "We will call your parents and send a plane to Dagestan. Tonight, you are flying back to the Netherlands. Please hand the telephone to Sergey again."

Me: "Who did I talk with?"

Cheerful Russian: "With Onno. You see that it's all true?"

The men saw a change in my behavior. Moments later, I got the phone pressed in my hands again.

Sergey: "The ambassador."

Me: "It is Arjan."

Ambassador: "Tido Hofstee. I am so happy to hear from you. We have been so worried."

I was a little perplexed that I had the ambassador on the line. I did not know how to address him. Is it Ambassador, sir, or excellency?

Ambassador: "Just a little while, and you can go home."

Me: "How are my parents?"

Ambassador: "Everyone is doing well. I am going to call them right away. Everyone will be so happy."

Me: "Yes, it is over. Life starts again."

Ambassador: "The plane will land at noon, and I will pick you up from the airport in Moscow."

Me: "Good. See you later."

The big Russian guy took the phone back and immediately gave it back to me. "It is DWB."

DWB: "Hello, this is Steve. Hey mate, how are you?"

Me: "I am doing fine. Do we know each other?"

DWB: "Yes, I worked for a few months in Sierra Leone as a country manager at DWB-France when you also worked there."

Me: "Oh, yes, we beat you playing soccer."

DWB: "Do you remember that? How is it going? Congratulations! We are coming to pick you up."

I wanted to call my parents and Amina, but they denied my request. My release had to remain a secret to everyone in Dagestan.

The cheerful Russian started to question me, but I did not want to answer.

Cheerful Russian: "Do not be silly. We risked our lives to get you out, and now you are protecting your abductors."

Me: "Maybe so, but I did not want to tell my story three times. Surely there will be time for one questioning soon?"

Cheerful Russian: "Good, we will do that later. Let's go to the hotel."

They dropped me at the FSB office in the middle of Makhachkala. I recognized the building when we walked to the car. It was already getting light, and we drove past my old flat towards the airport. We turned into the FSB's country retreat.

Sergey: "Take a nice bath. I bought new clothes for you."

The big Russian gave me clean underpants, soap, and a toothbrush with toothpaste.

Me: "It is not needed. I washed my clothes yesterday. I have toothpaste and a toothbrush."

Sergey: "No problem. Go take your shower."

Me: "Shall I shave my beard?"

Sergey: "No, you better wait a bit. With a beard, you will look more impressive."

It was terrific to use running water for the first time in 20 months. I sang many songs out loud and took a long bath. It was unreal, and I tried to cry, but I could not. When I let the water run out, a dirty, greasy, thick, yellow stripe remained on the bathtub. I quickly washed it away.

The men arranged breakfast, and we sat on the balcony. My first sunrise was fantastic. The sun was just rising over the Caspian Sea.

Sergey: "It is Easter. For the first time in years that Orthodox and Catholic Easter coincide, a sign from God. Take another piece of cake. My mother baked it, especially for you."

They started again with a light interrogation.

Sergey: "Have you agreed on a possible interrogation?"

Me: "Yes, that will take place in Moscow. You do not have to question me here."

I told the men to wait until Moscow with their questions. I told them some things but not any details.

A female doctor performed a medical examination. She looked at my finger and concluded that I did not have a break in it. She could not say much about my guts, either. According to her, it was nothing serious.

We left for the airport at noon, and Sergey bought me a bottle of Dagestani cognac. We drove to the plane that waited on the runway. Steve and two unknown men stepped out of the airplane. One of them was Onno, the diplomat, and Valentin Velichko, the director of the KGB Veterans Society. We embraced and took some photos. On the two-hour flight to Moscow, I received a briefing. Onno, Velichko, and Steve briefed me about what happened in twenty months of captivity. The information did not sink in. Luckily, Steve brought some of my clothes. I took a close look at the gorgeous stewardesses. After all, I did not see any women for 607 days. A DWB doctor examined me again.

In Moscow, the ambassador waited for me, and I embraced him. The friendly diplomat gave me an awkward hug. Probably he did not hug a lot during the official visits. On the way to his car, a photographer followed us. When I sat in the back seat, the photographer asked me to clench my fist and cheer. The car was a big Volvo with Dutch flags on the front of the hood. During the drive through Moscow, I finally relaxed. In Dagestan and on the plane, I feared an assassination attempt to get rid of me as a witness. Steve, the ambassador, and I prepared a press statement. They expected a lot of press in the street in front of the embassy. And to protect me, they would not let me speak to the media freely. The ambassador, his wife, and Steve and his wife Madina welcomed me. Mrs. Hofstee's scales showed that I lost 42 pounds. I showered again.

I made my first phone call to my mother. As expected, she was incredibly happy and surprised that I endured so well. I was a happy child, but I muted my emotions. I experienced difficulty to express my real feelings. She asked if I would like to be welcomed in their new hometown Westdorpe as an Olympic champion.

Me: "Why in Westdorpe? We are from Rotterdam; you just moved to Westdorpe three years ago?"

Mother: "The people from the village have been so involved all the time. The village council and mayor have proposed a warm welcome for you here."

Me: "Mayor Opstelten from Rotterdam did not call?"

Mother: "No, not yet."

Me: "Do you want a party tonight?"

Mother: "If we do it tomorrow, there will be more time to invite everyone."

It did not matter to me. I found it difficult to make choices. Esther, my oldest brother's girlfriend, also came online. Afterward, I called my sister, but she did not answer. I left a voice message that I was disappointed that she switched off her phone on such an important day. I contacted her through my brother. She was full of joy and said several times that she loves me so much. As my brother and sister traveled to my parent's house with their partners, Minou and Casper, I talked to my oldest brother and father in their car on their way to the airport. My father flew to Moscow tonight to pick me up. Finally, I called my friend Olaf. He was with his mother. After I told my story quickly, he proudly told me he had a daughter. Also, he said to me that my favorite soccer team Feyenoord played to a draw against Ajax, the rival team from Amsterdam.

I was expected outside at 6 p.m. for a press conference. I was nervous about my press debut. Journalists packed the street. I intended to enjoy my "15 minutes of fame." Unfortunately, this was not the case. Mr. Hofstee and Steve did not want me to say anything more than the prepared statement. I did not like the loss of my freedom. Back in the house, colleagues and acquaintances trickled in. Everyone was happy to see me. I enjoyed the attention, but I had been awake for more than fifty hours. I called Amina. She was overjoyed and burst into tears. I also made a phone call to Khadji Murrat, the driver who was with me when I got kidnapped. He was happy and cried, as well.

I was so occupied, and I had so many new impressions that I did not have time to process my emotions. Or did it have to do with my defense mechanism not to come across emotionally?

On Teletext, I read the messages about my release, and I watched the news. There was a special news bulletin in the Netherlands to report my release. Even CNN reported my release. I dreamt about how journalists might forget my case, but now I was on the world's biggest news channel.

I asked if it was possible to wait for my father in a private room at the airport. I wanted to be by ourselves the moment we met. When he entered, we dove into each other's arms and let our tears run free. Of course, he looked a bit older than before, but luckily the hardship did not show on his face.

In the plane provided by the Dutch Air Force, I talked for hours with my father.

My father told me of the impact and attention paid to my abduction in the Netherlands and worldwide. Even President Bush, the Pope, and President Putin knew about my situation. At home, my family and friends were distraught, but luckily everyone was doing fine. My father and brother

Diederik met Amina and her parents in Moscow. My family was upset about DWB and did not want any contact with them. I noticed that my father did not say a word to Steve, who flew with me at my request.

I met the director of Consular Affairs of the Ministry of Foreign Affairs, Willem Andreae. He had worked on my release for twenty months. He was also happy that I was back again. I understood to what extent people had worked on my case.

For the third time today, I was examined by a doctor. He canceled the idea of taking me to a hospital immediately upon arrival.

I felt dazed. Everything went so fast. Last night I was walking through the mountains, and now I was about to land in the Netherlands.

We arrived at Rotterdam Airport in the middle of the night. The airport closed at 11 pm. But they permitted us to land for this special occasion.

At the bottom of the airplane stairs, I saw my family waiting. First, I embraced my mother. It looked like her arms were longer than usual. Her face was full of happiness. Then I walked towards my younger brother, but my sister, Roos, stepped between us and gave me a long hug. One by one, I hugged everyone and even kissed the ground. It was overwhelming. On the way to the arrival building, I quickly shook hands with a man I believed was the airport director.

"Who was that?" I asked Roos. "That was the Minister of Foreign Affairs, Ben Bot. He paid your ransom." I decided to go back just to shake his hand again. How was I supposed to know his position and role? I had been away for almost two years.

In a room in the airport building, we drank champagne while enjoying one of my favorite African songs. I chose a beer myself. It did not taste as expected, and I did not finish it. It seemed as if the entire Dutch press had gathered in the arrival hall. I stepped into the hall and was overwhelmed with questions and cameras. I told them that I was incredibly happy to be back. I showed them my beard and stammered that it was a pity that Feyenoord played to a draw against Ajax. I answered some questions, embraced friends, and then stepped out of the hall. Because journalists chased my family like paparazzi, airport security exited us unnoticed. While at my sister's house, I decided to shave my beard. My family was dying for answers about my time as a hostage. They showed me the newspaper clippings about my case in the Netherlands. Fortunately, my sister used a nice picture of me for communication matters. On the shirts, posters, cards, and in newspapers, I saw a nice photo taken in Antwerp.

After hours of talking, we all went to sleep, relieved and happy. I laid down on my own in the bedroom and wondered if I should bring a bottle to urinate. Do not be silly, I thought to myself. I could go to the toilet at any time. Due to too much adrenaline, I had trouble falling asleep. Eventually, I felt a shiver from the top of my head to the tip of my toes. I felt all the spiritual dirt washed from me. I was safe again!

The craziness continued in the morning. At three o'clock, my parents expected me in Westdorpe. It was a two-hour drive, so we left Rotterdam at 12.30. We had to hurry. Journalists waited on the phone with requests for interviews. Family and friends called with congratulations. It took some time to find something nice from my brother in law's wardrobe. Because I lost 42 pounds, I did not fit in my clothes.

Westdorpe wanted to honor me with a drive through the village in a convertible. A brass band accompanied us through town. I had never lived there, and my parents moved to Westdorpe three years ago. But I knew the place because my parents used to have a holiday house there. It was a friendly place. Along the way, we stopped to refuel and buy the Sunday edition of the biggest newspaper. My picture with a beard in the ambassador's car's back seat was on the front page.

In Westdorpe, we met as planned at the fire department. A red Mercedes convertible and driver were waiting for me, but otherwise, the streets were almost empty. Did it make sense to be driven through empty streets?

"People are gathering in the center," said the driver. "Just look." I sat down in the back, and the car slowly drove towards the main street. Along the way, I was happy to see some family members who greeted me warmly and were excited to see me. Closer to the main street, the road had more crowds. Children gave me drawings, and strangers gave me flowers. The crowd size impressed me and did not know what else to do other than waving. Dozens of journalists pushed their microphone under my nose and asked the same thing.

"How do you feel now? What do you think of this tour? Are you happy to be back? What is going through your mind?"

How can a professional athlete calmly answer the same questions year after year?

A crowd of several thousand people blocked the main street. I gave and received hugs from people I knew. The brass band played music, and slowly but surely, we approached my parent's house. Family and friends were there waiting. I urged them to sing a song that we always sang at weddings and parties. I got out of the car and greeted and kissed everyone. The members of the organizing committee looked anxiously at their watches. My friend Olaf suggested we sneak out and go to a bar.

After speeches from the chairman of the village council and the mayor, it was my turn. I could not find words for a long speech but managed to thank the DWB, the Ministry of Foreign Affairs, the people present, and all Dutch people for their support and the press for the attention they devoted to my case.

After the welcome festivities, there was a press conference. And then it was finally time to dive into the pub. After twenty months of loneliness, I was now in the middle of a partying crowd. I loved seeing so many family, friends, and acquaintances. All this attention was right for me, and I wanted to talk to everyone.

After the party, we all ate dinner at my parent's house. Everyone enjoyed a great day. We watched the news and other TV programs, and I accepted my 15 minutes of fame. I guessed the attention would soon stop.

Satisfied, I drove back to Rotterdam with Roos and Casper. After two days of being pampered by my sister, and some mental and medical checkups, I wanted to go to my apartment to listen to the song Oerend Hard by Normaal.

The song was about the two notorious motorcyclists who drove around like crazy until a drunk driver hits them. After this accident, no one ever heard from them again. Although they will never ride fast again, the people around them will.

During the first months of my abduction, I ignored the lyrics. Later I thought I might have picked the wrong song. Would I die as well and never live a fast life anymore, or would I continue with a need for speed when I get out? I should have chosen a song with a good ending.

Together with Roos, we entered the place. The beautiful old wooden floor creaked as usual. Dozens of bouquets cheer up my living room. My house embraced me! Yes, I was home again. Immediately I walked over to my record player and played the song. My tears flowed over my cheeks. I listened in silence to the song.

"But as always, all the good things come to an end.

Due to a drunken guy who doesn't know the speed of a motorbike.

Bertus rode ahead, and Tinus came close behind.

And everyone said those guys will never be heard again.

They will never ever go fast again. They never, never ever go fast again

But we will speed up. We will need the speed. Need for speed again."

Yes, I survived. I will live on, I said to myself. I saw myself singing this song in my little, dark, wooden prison cell to keep up my courage. While at the same time doubting if I would get out alive.

There was a religious dimension to my release at Easter. I felt my freedom as a type of resurrection. I did not yet know how my life would turn out.

Would my life be *"Oerend hard"*, ridiculously fast? The future would come later. There were various offers from publishers among the thousands of letters and e-mails. Maybe when the first rush was over, I would write a book about my experiences.

Epilogue

When I just landed in Rotterdam, I had a little conversation with myself. Would I manage to go back to regular everyday life, or would I carry my experience's heavy toll?

During my kidnapping, I excelled and surprised myself, surpassed myself, and had more power and influence than I ever imagined. Why could I not do the same in freedom? Life as a free man would be more comfortable than in a hostage situation, for sure. So, I told myself that I didn't want to be taken hostage for the rest of my life.

My release happened on Easter, such a symbolic day, the day of resurrection of Jesus Christ. With a long beard just getting out of my cage, I could relate to Jesus' story very well. It felt that I got a second chance to make something out of my life.

In the first few months, I enjoyed being back. I met with my family and friends and made sure that mental health professionals and medical doctors checked my health.

My reintegration went exceptionally smoothly. With help from my family and friends, my life coach, and the support of many friendly Dutch people, I managed to pick up a stable life again. Of course, I appreciated their support, but life is not about gaining sympathy; instead, it is about overcoming and creating. I can advise all people not to hide or deny the hardship they experienced. I managed to interweave it in my life, which allowed me to accept my history. Vulnerability gives freedom, as well.

I wrote a best seller in The Netherlands as my first new project. I married Amina, my fiancée from Dagestan, and we have three lovely daughters: Anna, Arabella, and Adriana.

My life coach triggered me when he said that many people, figuratively speaking, are taken hostage or stuck in life, whether due to finances, health issues, broken love, lack of ambition or self-esteem, or upbringing.

I became a motivational speaker and entrepreneur. My kidnapping helped me increase my freedom in daily life and gave me much more strength and courage to start and finish all kinds of projects that I did not even dream of creating. Since my dark period, I am more aware of my possibilities, resilience, discipline, and courage.

I would like those 20 months of misery to change and inspire other people to find their power to start a second life. I want my experience to be a catalyst and example for people to change for the better. So, I want people to move away from the wrong things in life and go in the direction of good things to influence them to think about freedom of choice and freedom to act.

My message is about increasing freedom and autonomy to connect with your real goals and act to reach them, demolishing your boundaries and beliefs that stand in the way. I see free agency, the power to choose, as the engine of innovation for others to unlock potential, happiness, and success.

I learned the hard way. You cannot always control your circumstances, but you can find the power inside yourself to make it through the dark places into the light. It helps to surround yourself with useful thoughts.

Now years later, I feel more compelled than ever to share my story. I am fortunate, my narrative has a happy ending, and good things have happened and are still happening.

Even now, as I write this book amid the uncertainty of the Coronavirus, where no one can be 100% sure of what tomorrow brings, it takes me firmly back to the days when I had to live each day, not knowing if I would live to see the next sunrise. I learned many lessons that helped me survive the experience.

Now, I enjoy life with my beautiful wife and three exceptional children. I want to share this message; never lose hope, and you can get through severe circumstances.

In the Netherlands, my story is well known, and I got the chance to inspire lots and lots of people. I even got the opportunity to speak in Singapore, New York, Aruba, Barcelona, London, and many other European places. My challenge is to think even bigger and go abroad more. Here is my book, Held Hostage, One Man's Story of Trials and Triumph After Being Taken in Dagestan.

I am a freedom fighter for two reasons. One because I activate people to look for mental freedom and to increase their freedom of choice.

My inspirational speaking sessions and Dutch books allowed me to meet so many exciting and inspiring people in many beautiful places. My story gave audiences worldwide a push in their backs to make a change for the better. I hope this book will find its way to many people to help them with one of the biggest challenges of life: to find freedom in one's mind.

Because of my ordeal, it became my mission to serve people in their search for freedom, to live in a world without fear, surrounded by protection.

Together with Evelien Hölsken, Roelof van Laar en Yolanthe Cabau, I founded Free a Girl. The international organization Free a Girl rescues minor-aged girls from sexual exploitation, empowers them, and fights impunity. Since the start, Free a Girl has rescued almost 5,000 children and put hundreds of perpetrators behind bars.

I am deeply grateful that I got a second chance, and I would like to be a voice for the 2 million trafficked children and the families who are still looking for their child.

Please feel free to donate to Free a Girl USA.

12 April 2004. One day after my release at a welcoming party in Westdorpe.

Reunited with family and friends

Meeting Queen Beatrix of The Netherlands

People in The Netherlands sent their best wishes.
Even postcards without address reached my home

Original book released in Dutch